Living On Memory Lane

Artist & Story Teller
Susan Curry

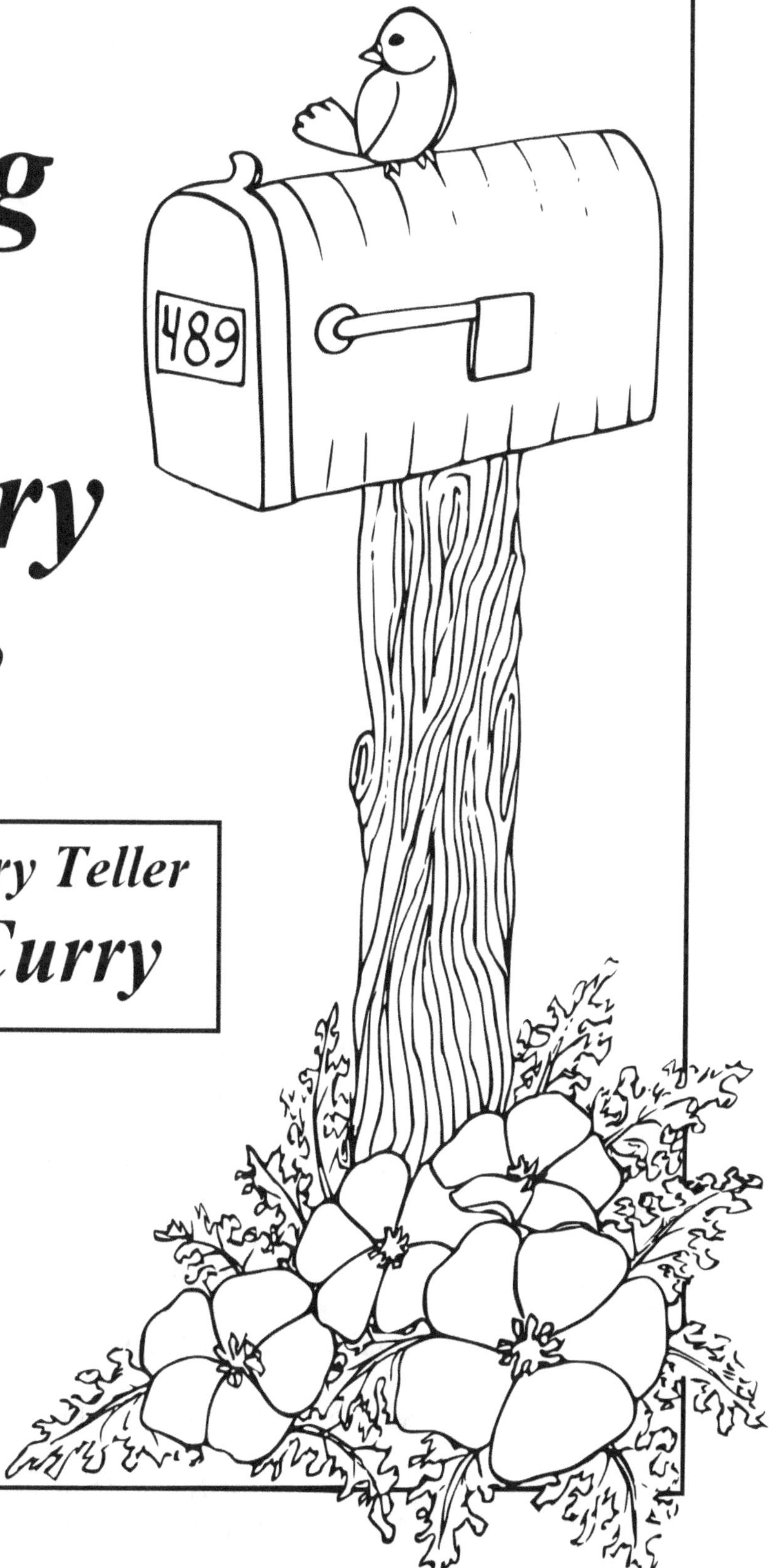

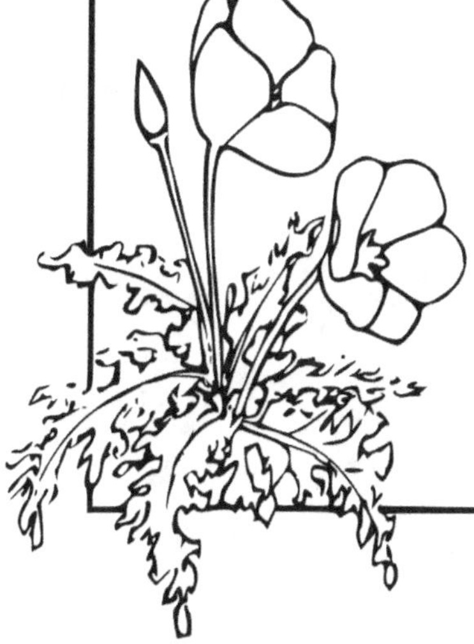

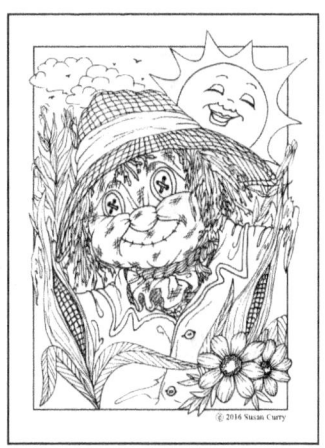

The Scarecrow

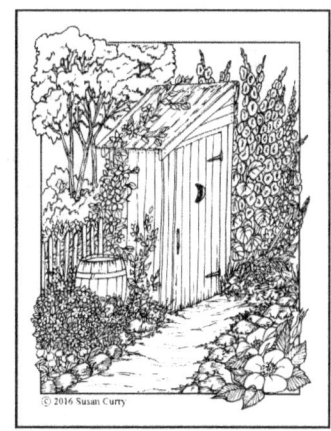

The Outhouse

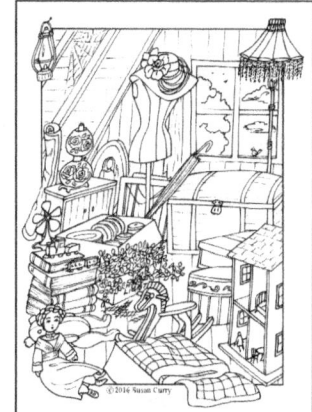

The Attic

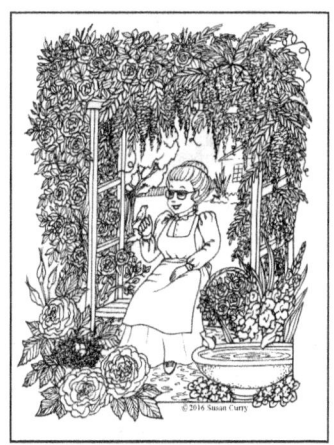

Nana's Flower Garden

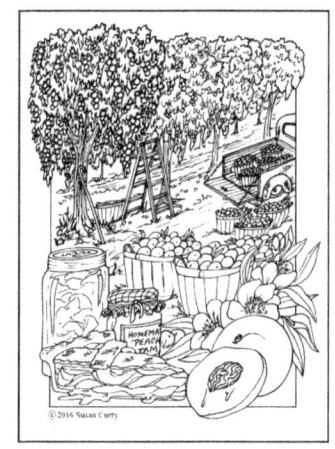

The Peach Harvest

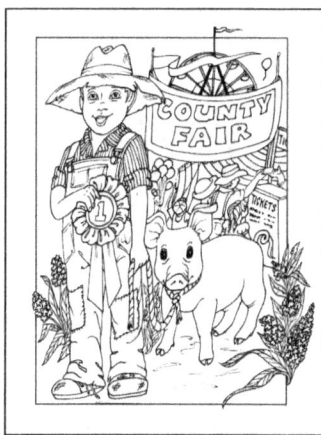

The Prize Winning Pig

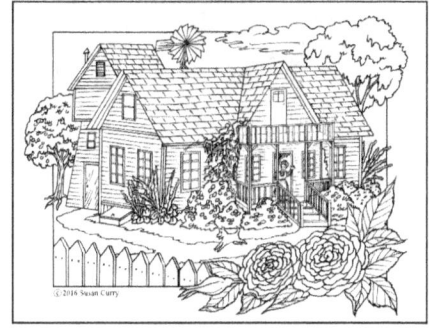

The Farmhouse

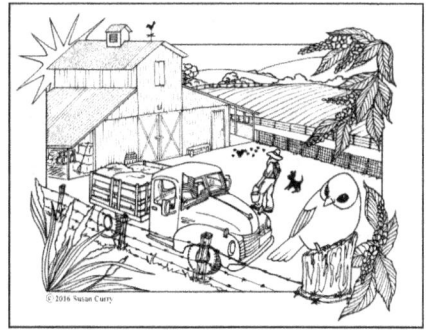

The Barn

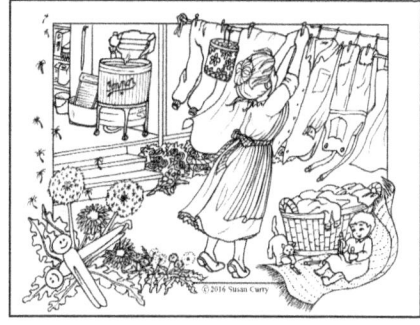

Laundry Day

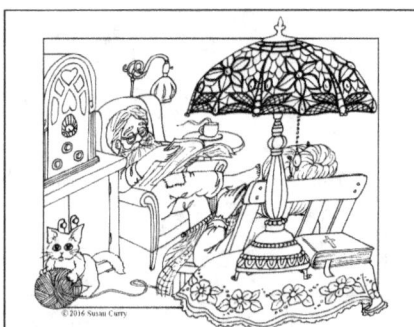

Listening To The Radio

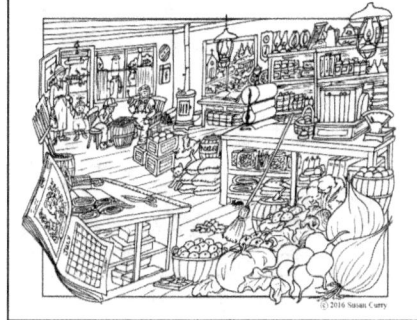

The General Store

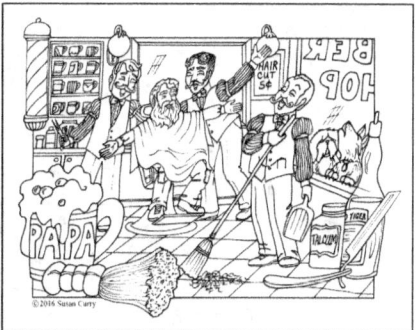

Sweet Adeline

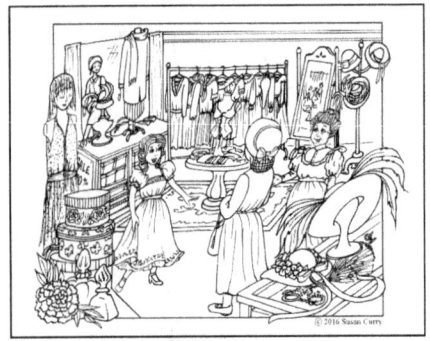

The Party Dress

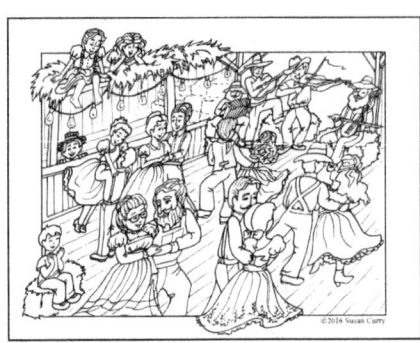

The Barn Dance

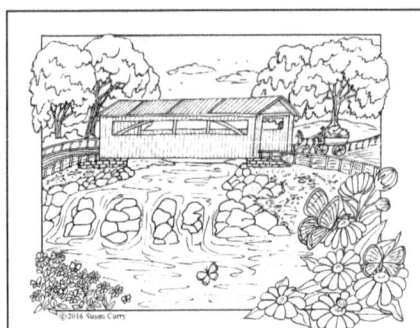

The Covered Bridge

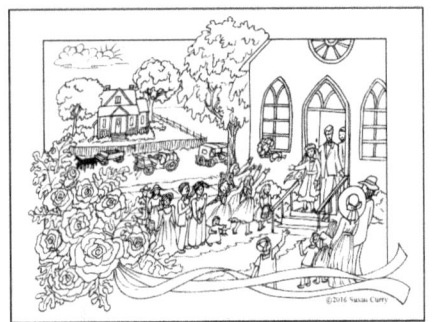

The Wedding Day

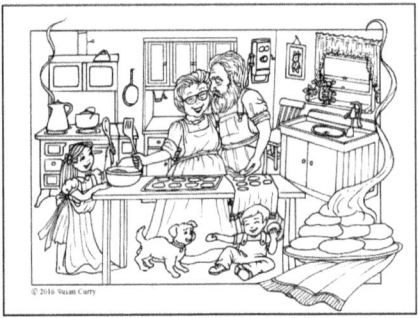

Warm Cookies

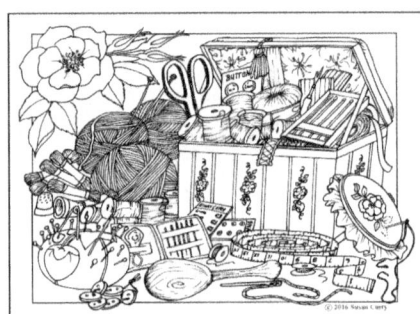

The Sewing Basket

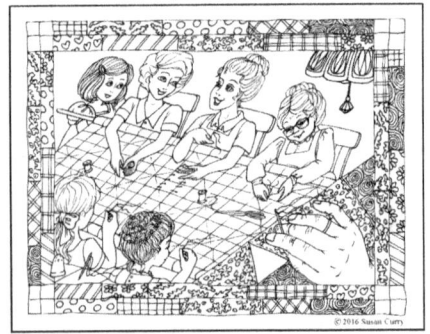

The Quilting Bee

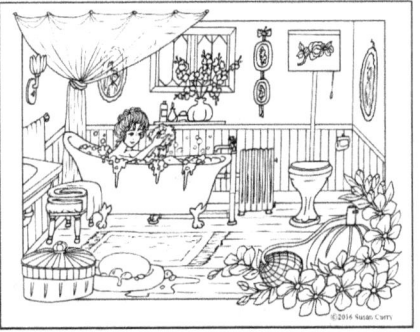

The Vintage Bathroom

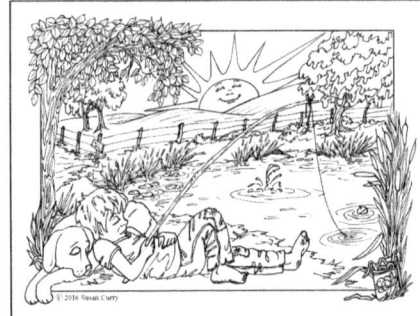

Gone Fishin'

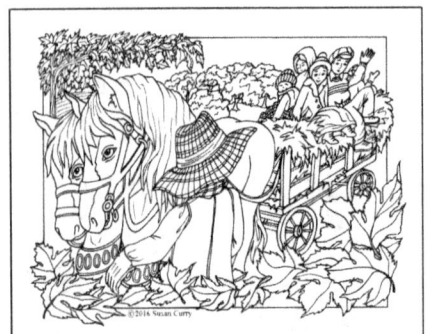

The Hay Ride

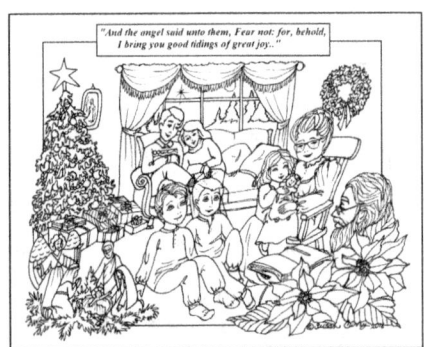

Christmas Eve

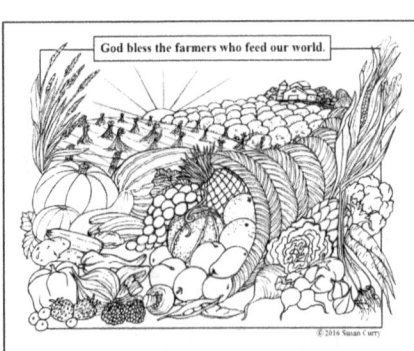

God Bless The Farmers

Dedication

This book would not have been possible without the help of 2 very special people.

My husband, Pastor Ed Curry is the love of my life; and he gave me his love and encouragement through out the creation of these drawings. His history as youngster growing up on a dairy farm, the stories of his family and his knowledge of that unique way of life were my inspiration for many of my drawings. He is my reference and guide in so many things. I thank God every day for putting him into my life.

My sweet friend and gifted artist, Christine Aldridge was the person who convinced me that 'I could draw again', as I had done in my younger days. She made me want to draw again. Without her constant encouragement and experience of 'making a coloring book', I would probably still be looking at my drawings and saying, "I can't do this." It was Christine who saw something in me that I could not. She literally put this book of drawings and writings together for all of you. I am so grateful for her generosity, help and friendship.

I want to also thank all of the great artists, colorists and online friends who encouraged me to create a coloring book for the first time. I hope that it will be worthy of all of you and will give you pleasure as you travel to a place called 'Memory Lane'.

* * * * *

IMPORTANT INFORMATION FOR USING THIS BOOK

- This book contains 24 hand-drawn illustrations, SINGLE SIDED (back is blank).

- Each illustration is printed in TWO SIZES, a full size page and a crafters size (suitable for a 5" x 7" frame, mounting to a greeting card face or scrapbook page, etc). Please note the crafters sizes are also single sided and are printed two on a page.

- The pages are printed on #60 lb bright white paper which performs well for all brands of colored pencils and crayons, without the need of a blotter page.

- To avoid any "Uh Oh's" and the associated disappointment, **Marker and Gel Pen users are STRONGLY ENCOURAGED to USE A BLOTTER SHEET** behind the drawing to avoid any possibility of bleed through to the next page.

- Most IMPORTANT of all: Relax, have fun, stand-up and stretch often, and remember that sometimes the most beautiful things come from what we think at first are mistakes, but which turn out to be art's way of working magic!

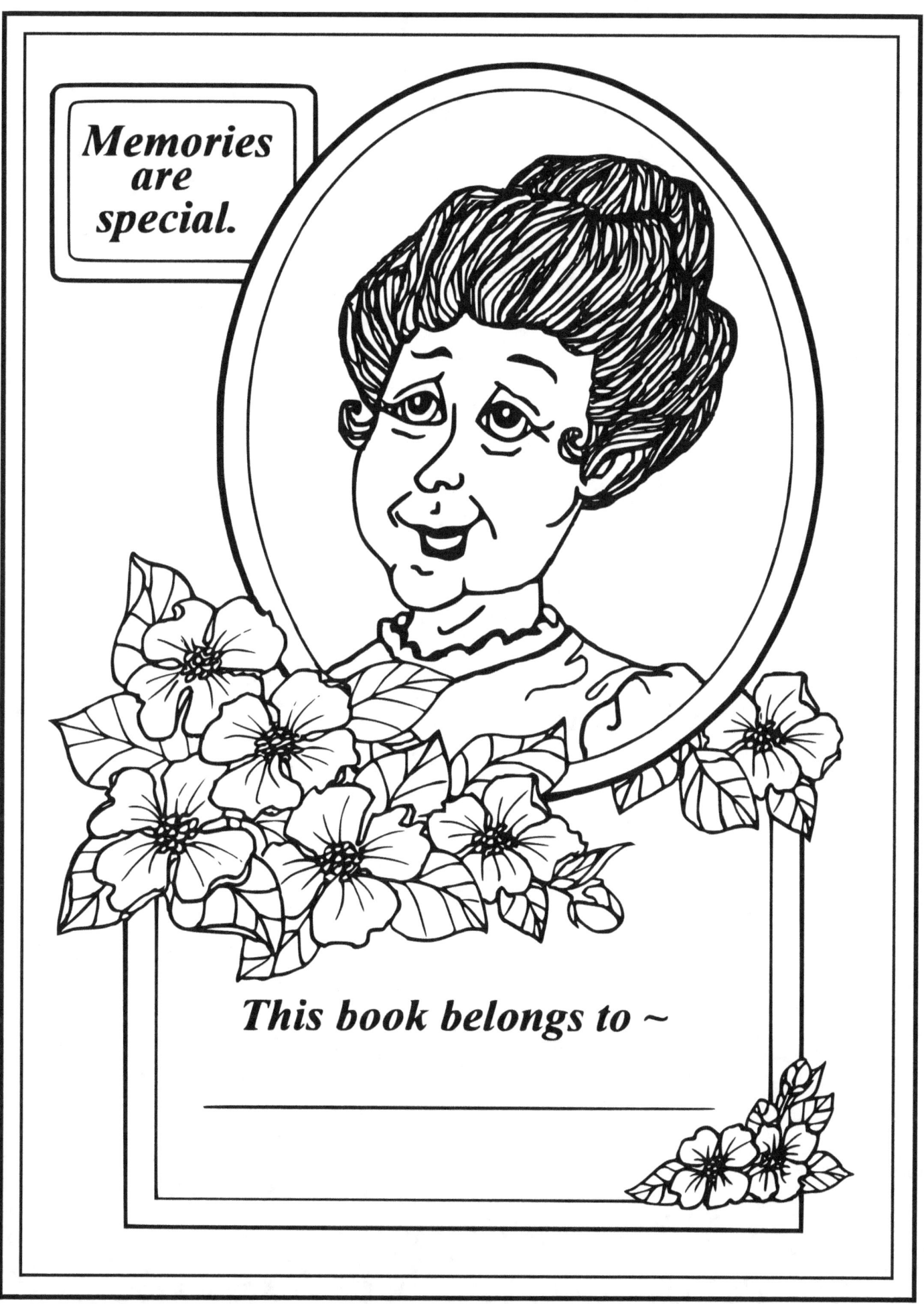

Memories
are
special.

This book belongs to ~

_____

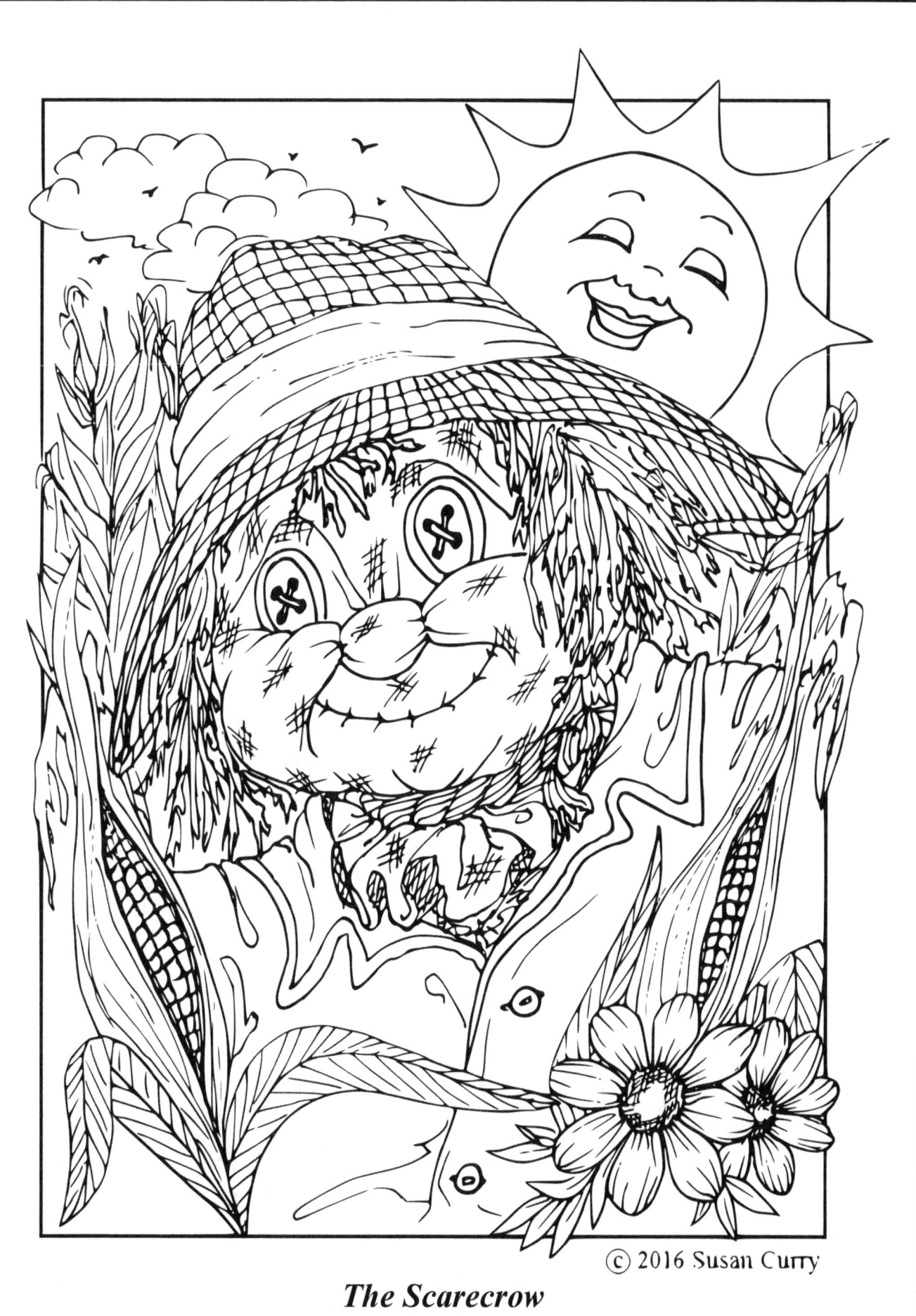

The Scarecrow

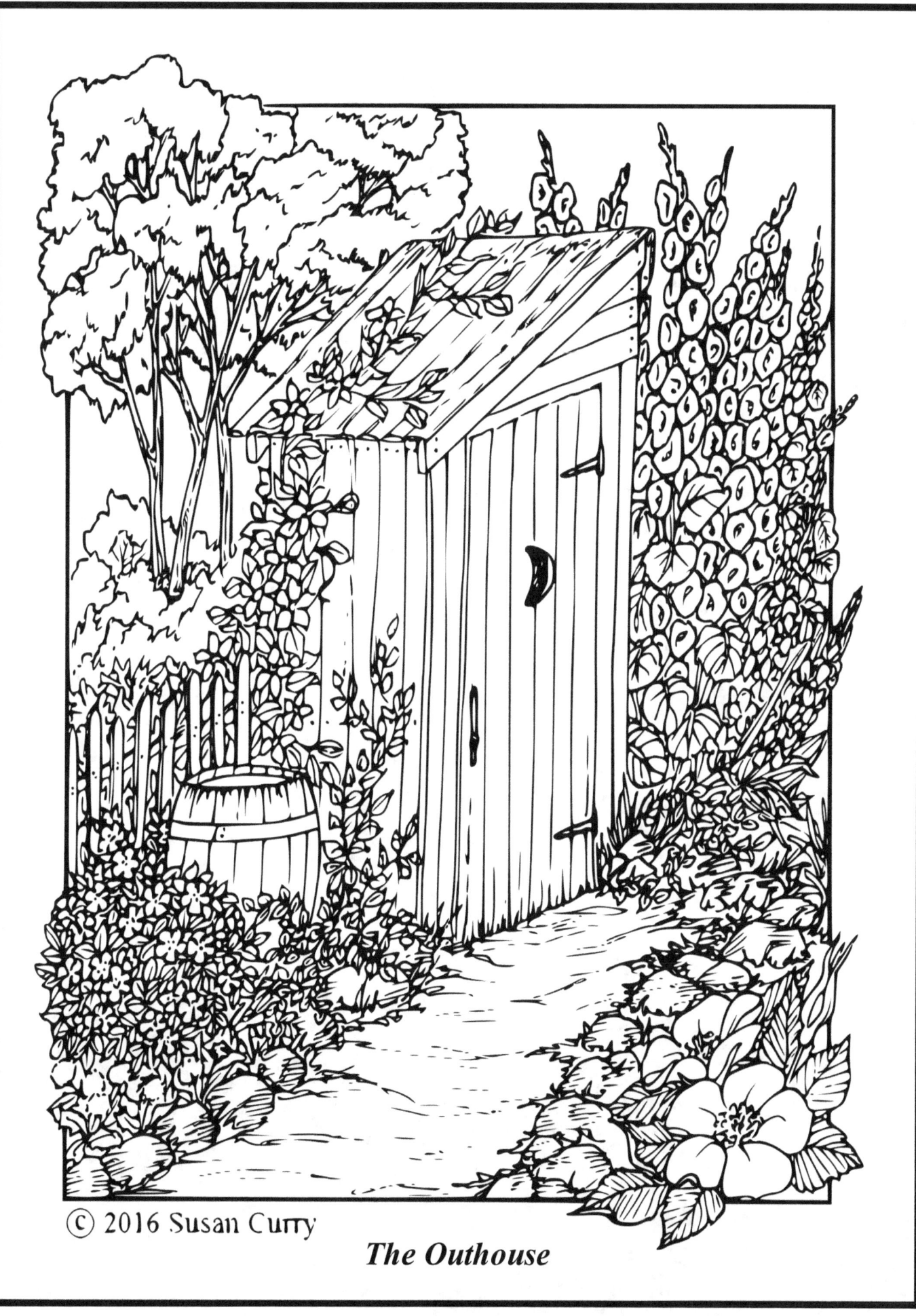

© 2016 Susan Curry

The Outhouse

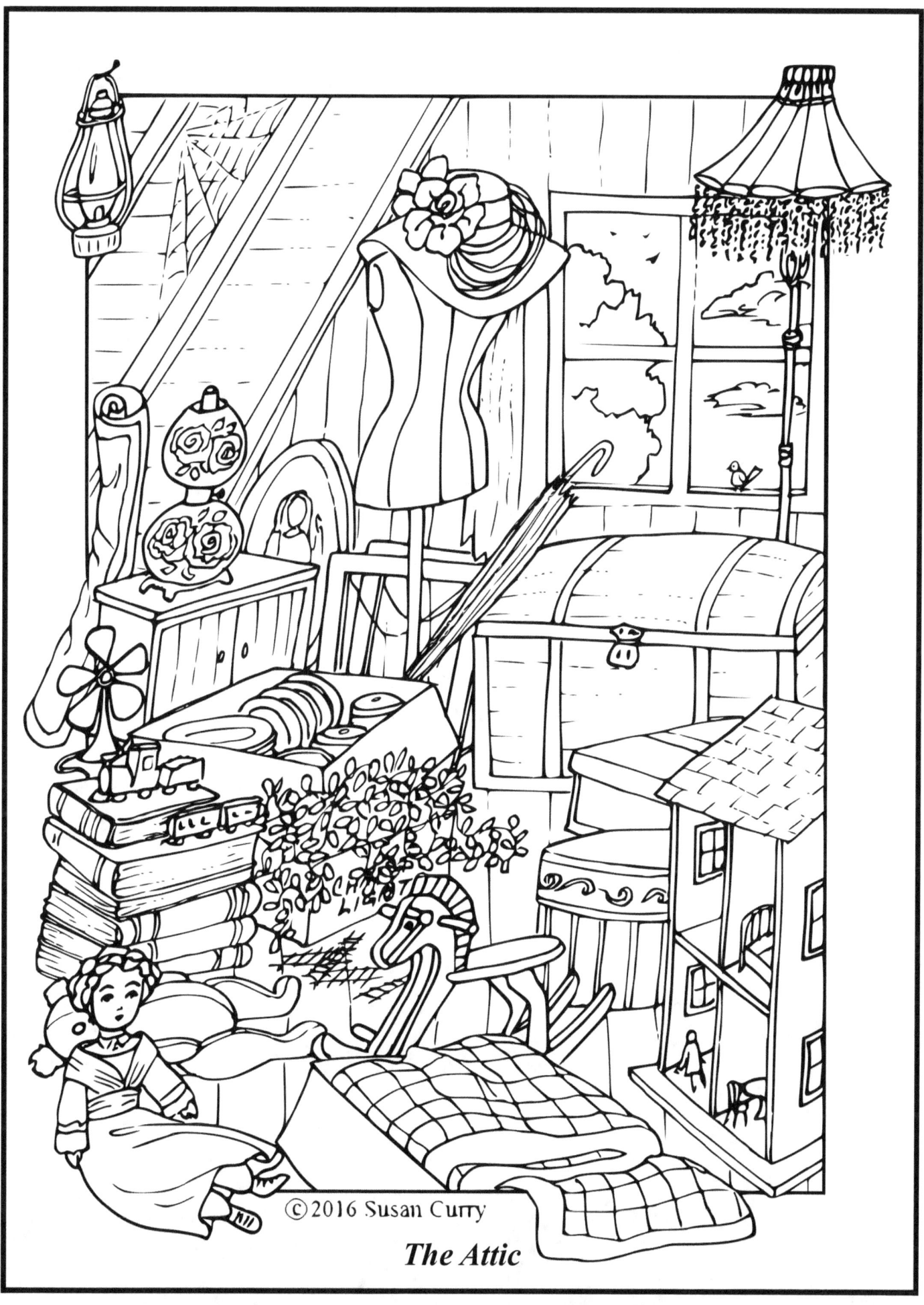

© 2016 Susan Curry

The Attic

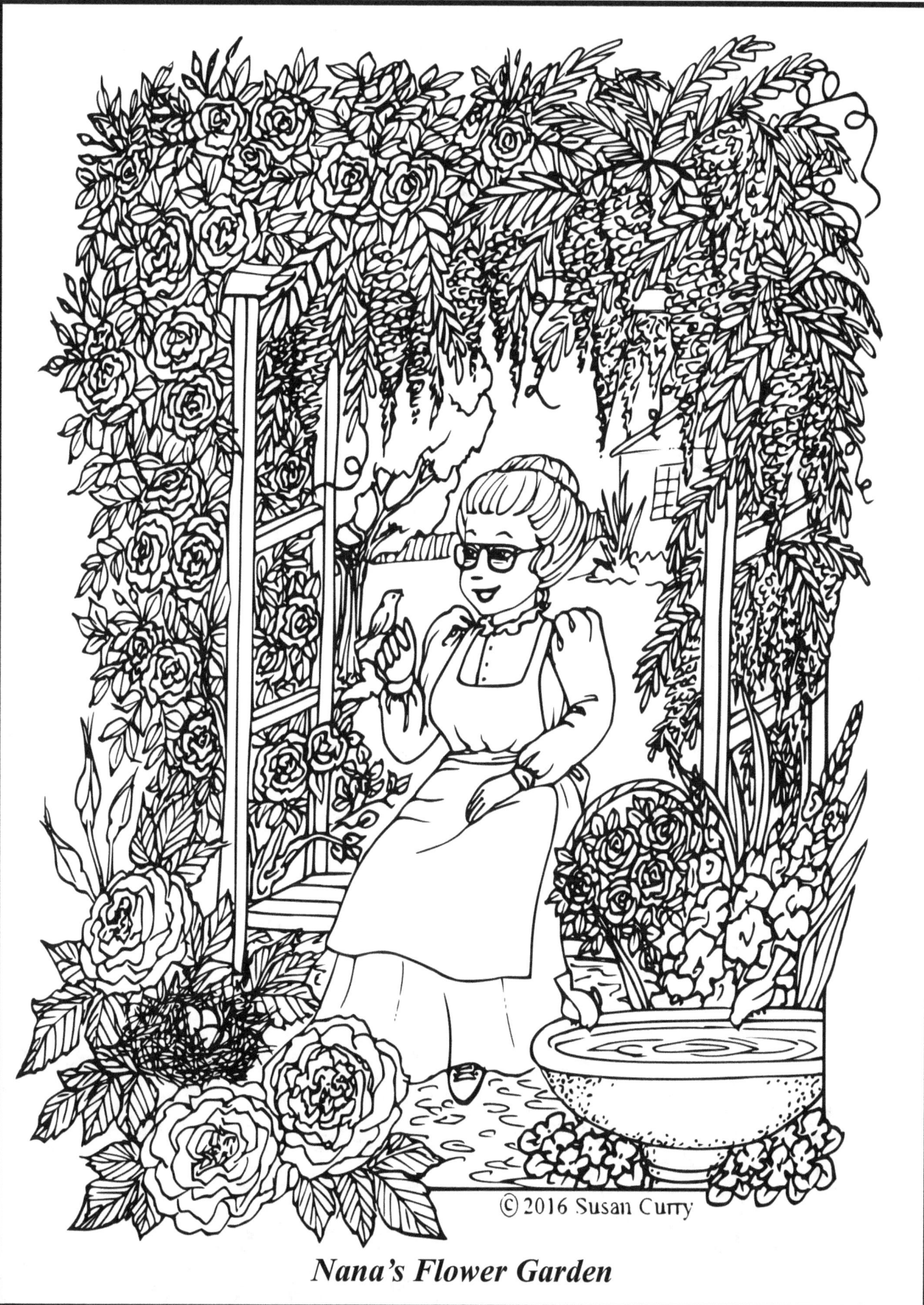

Nana's Flower Garden

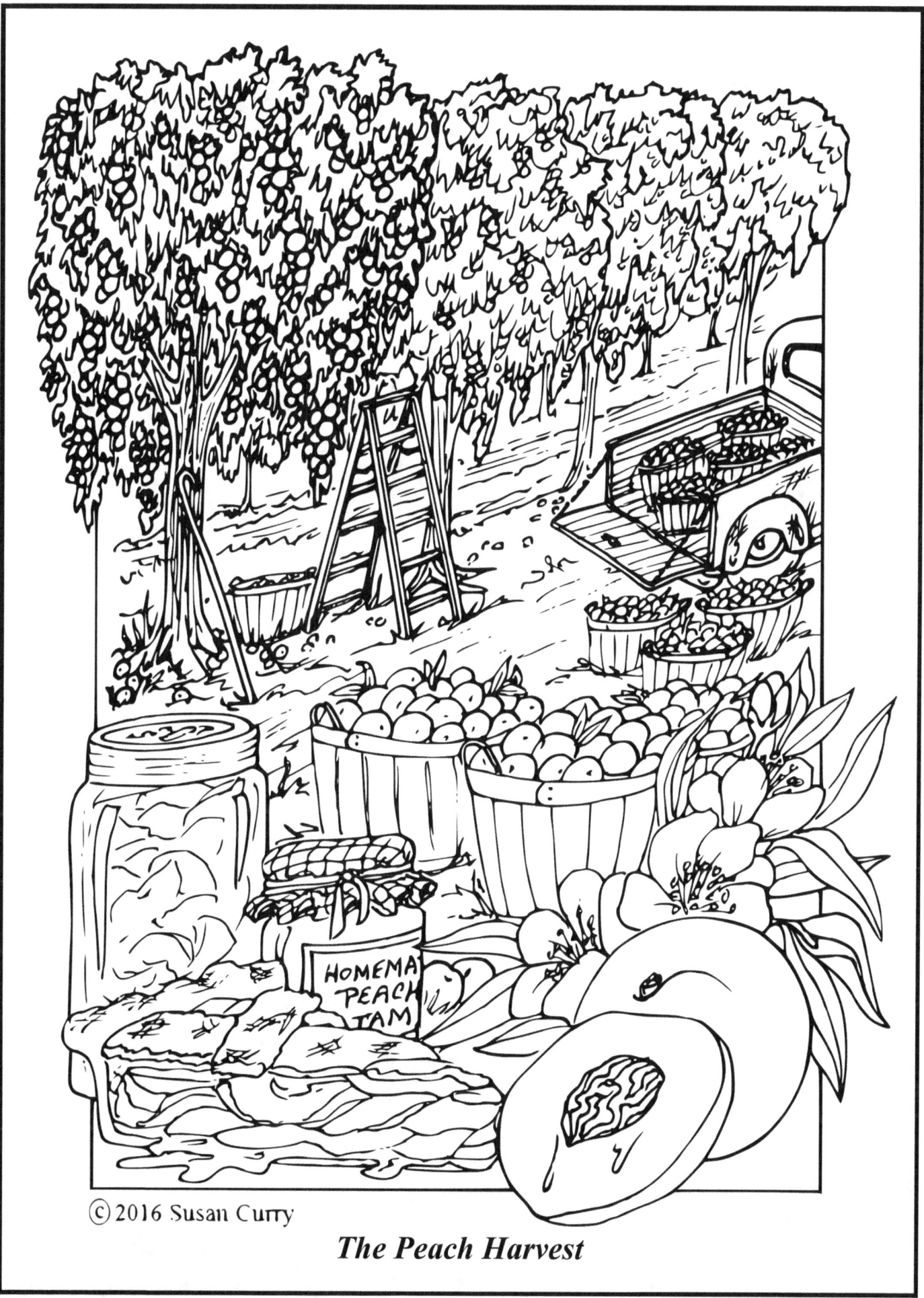

HOMEMA
PEACH
JAM

The Peach Harvest

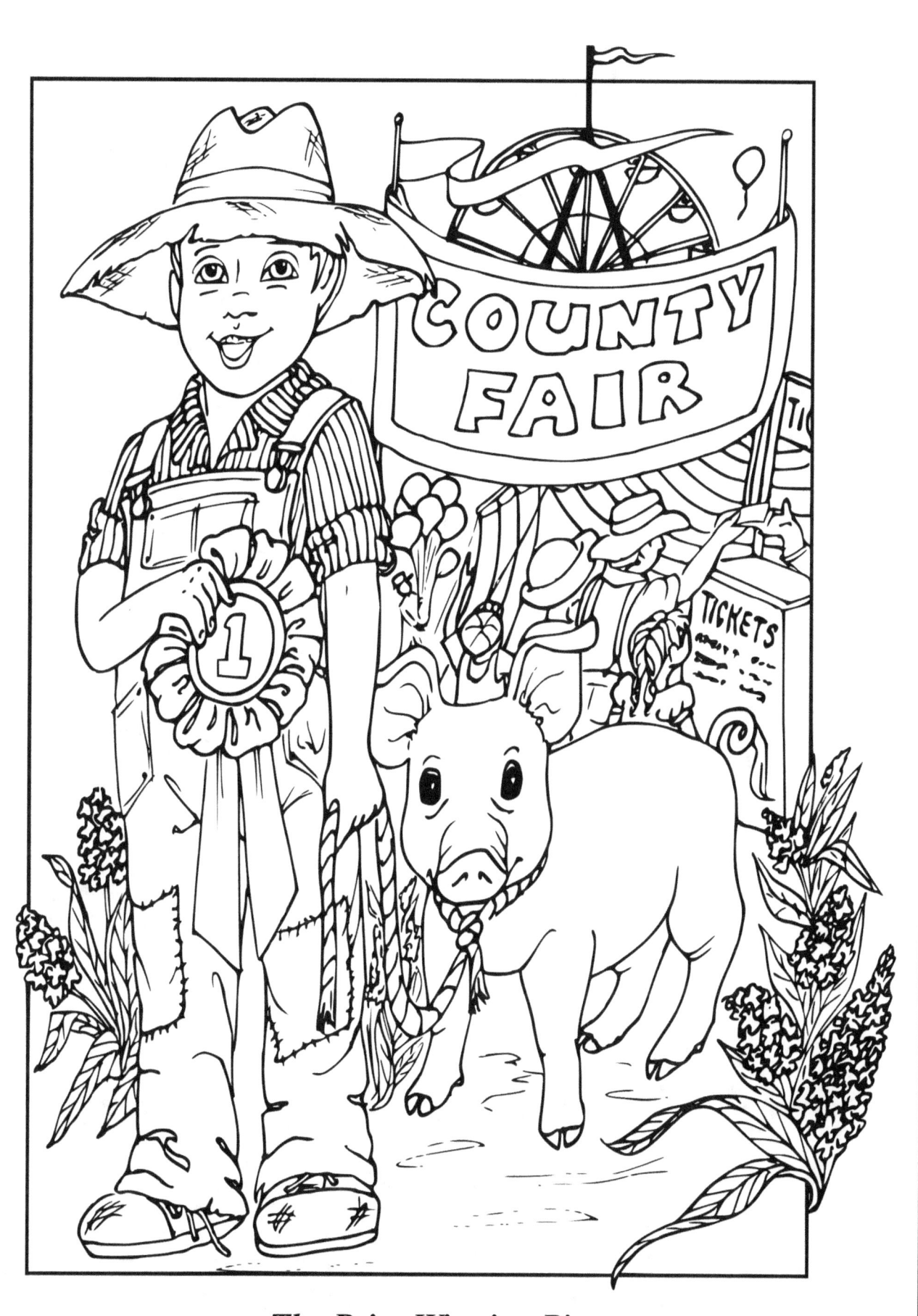

The Prize Winning Pig

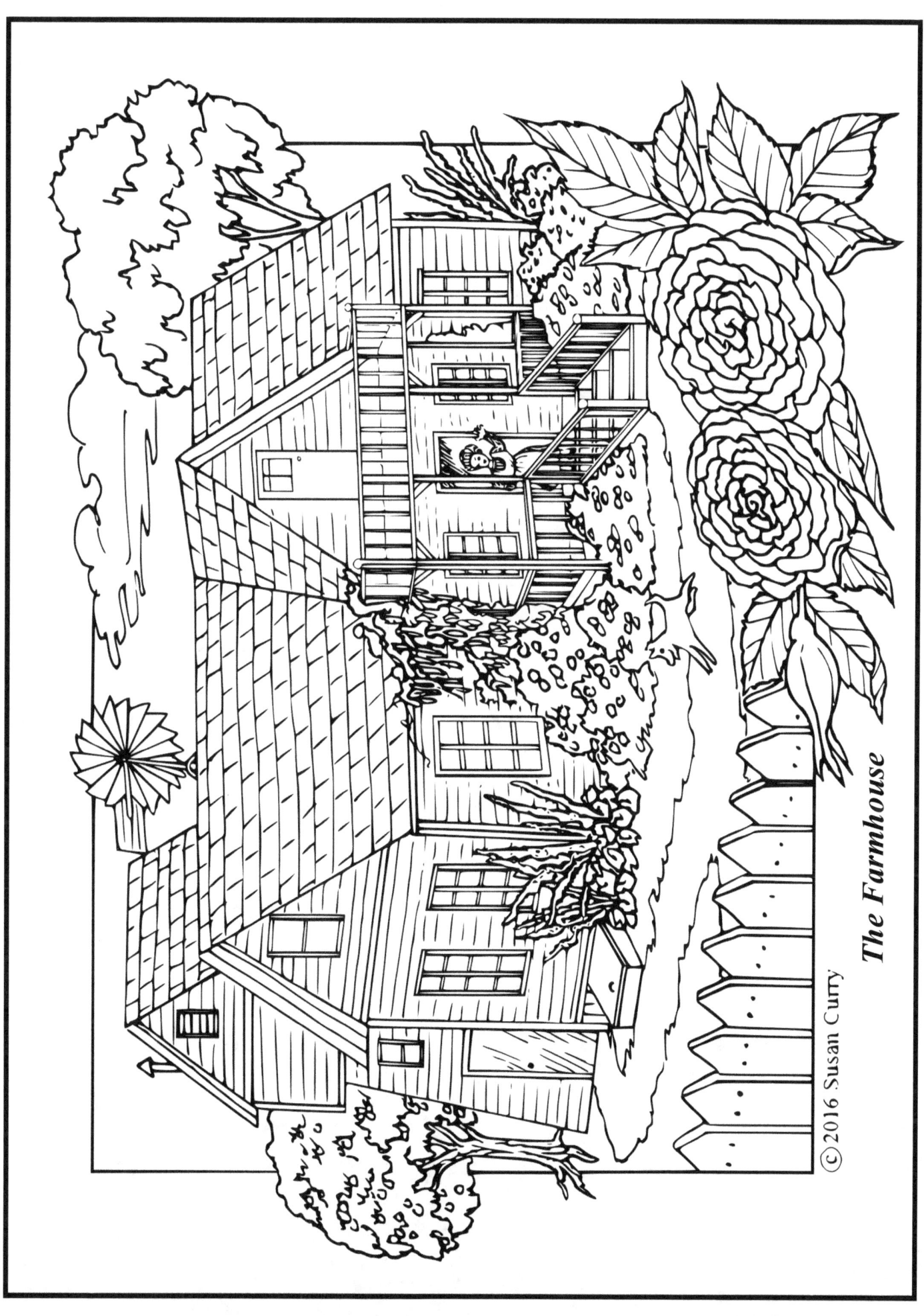

© 2016 Susan Curry

The Farmhouse

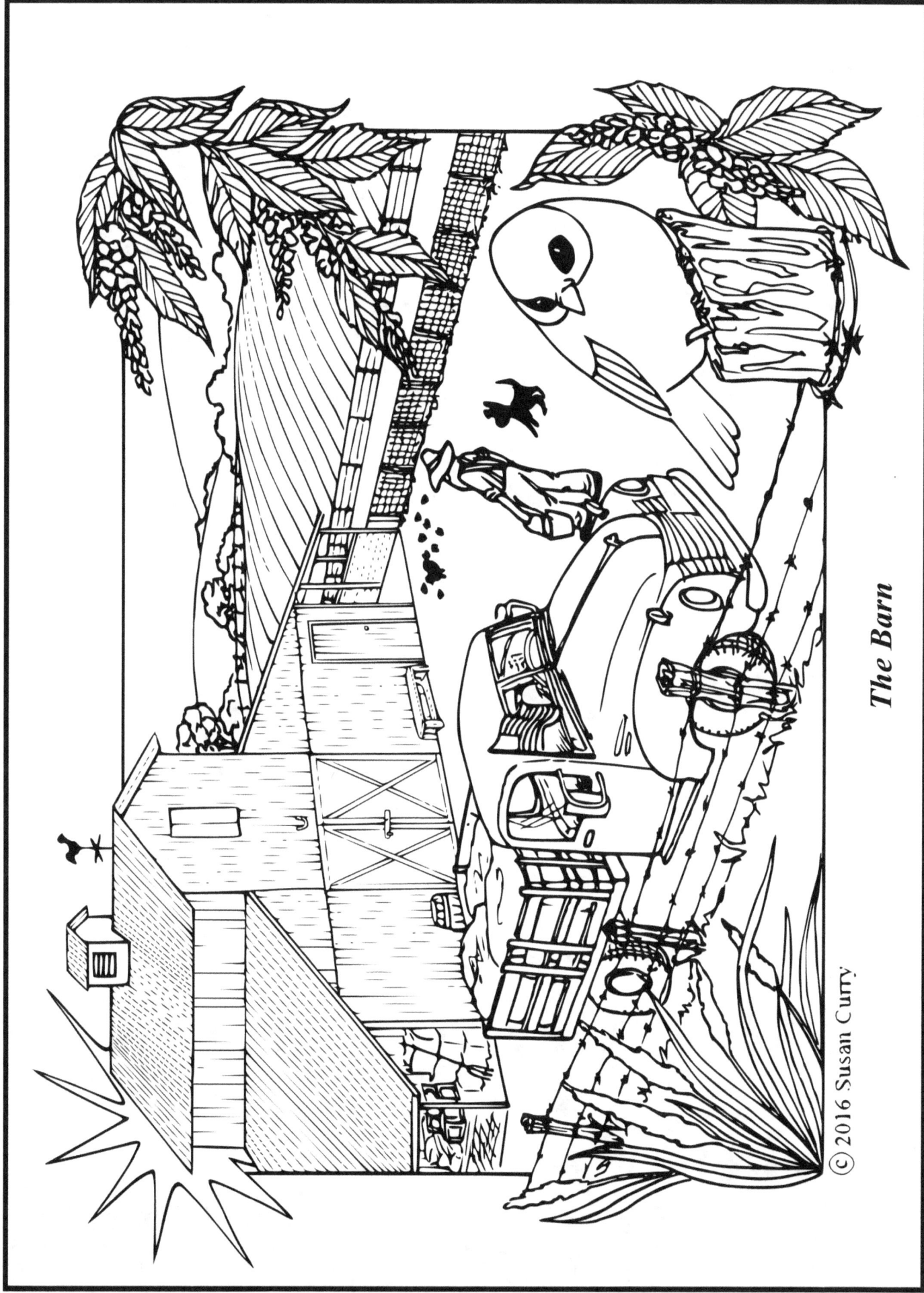

The Barn

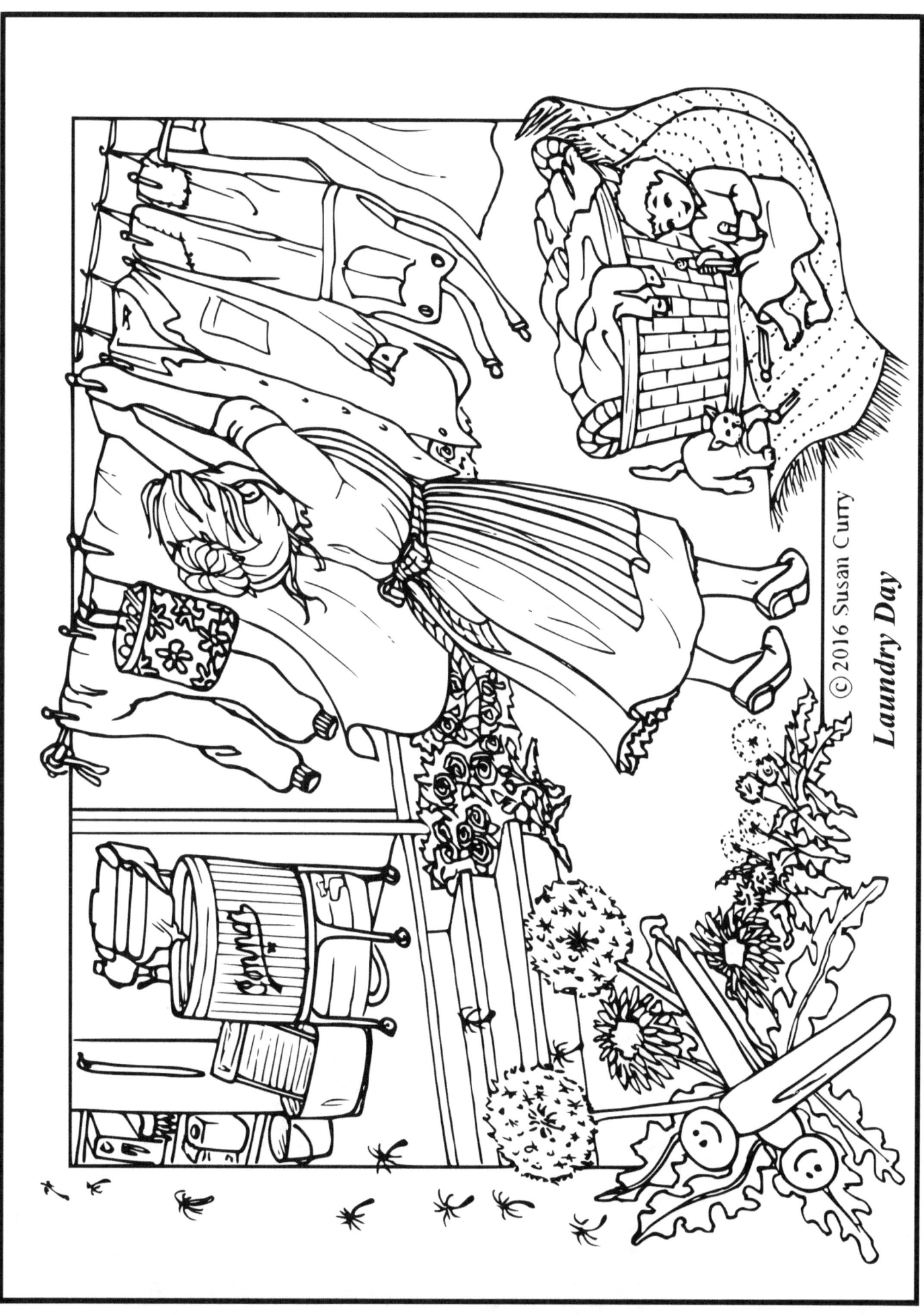

Laundry Day

© 2016 Susan Curry

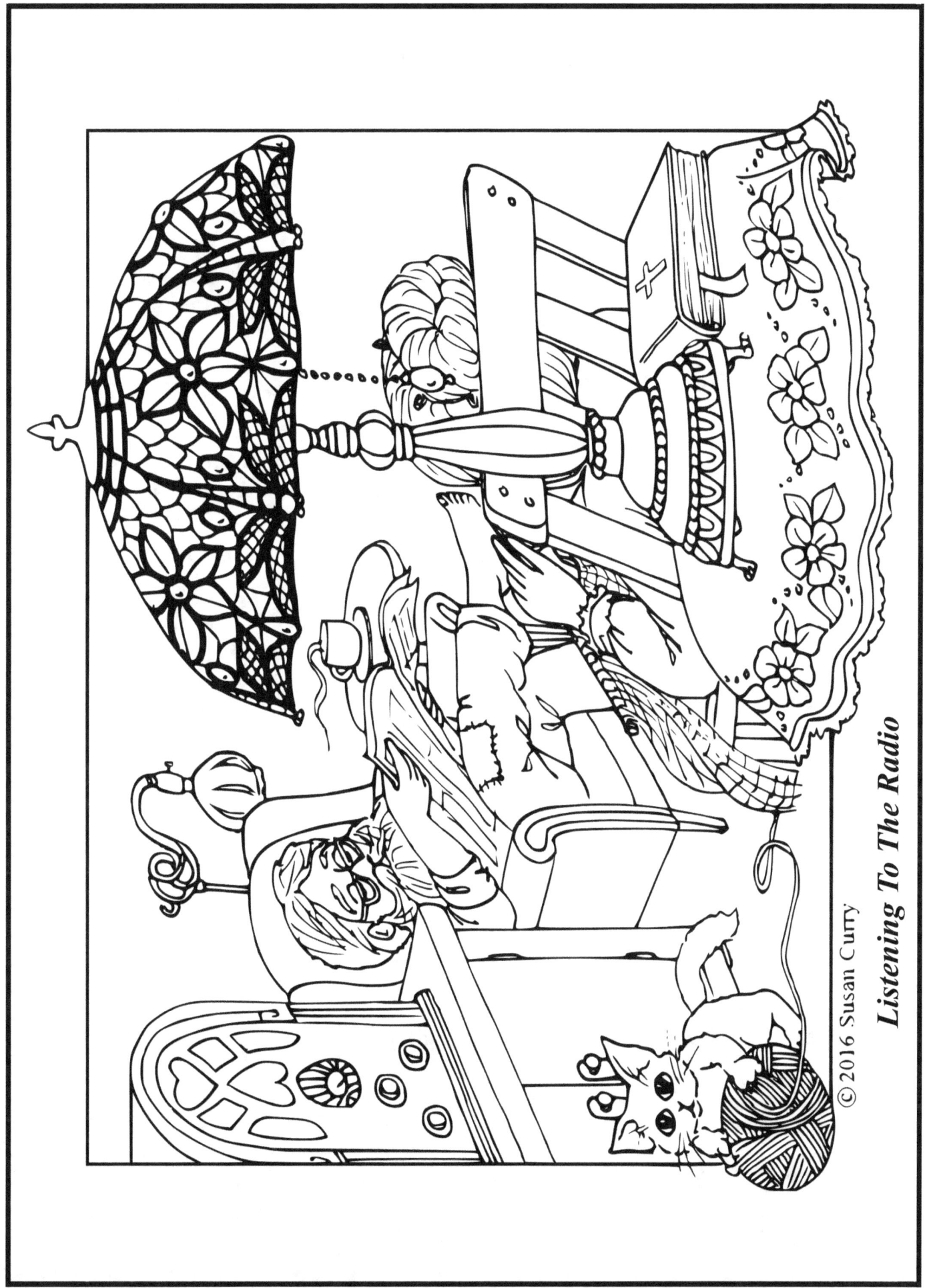

Listening To The Radio

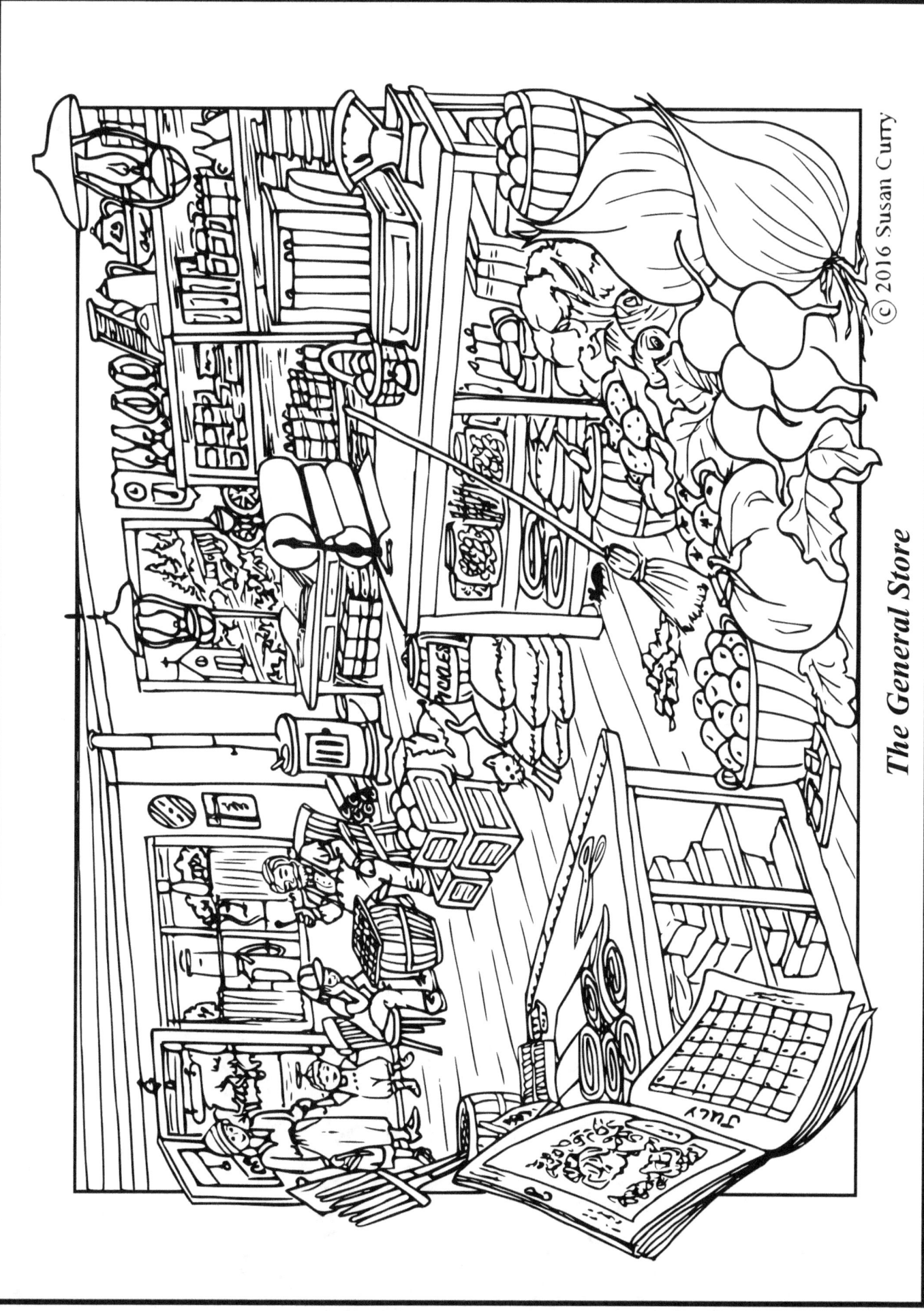

The General Store

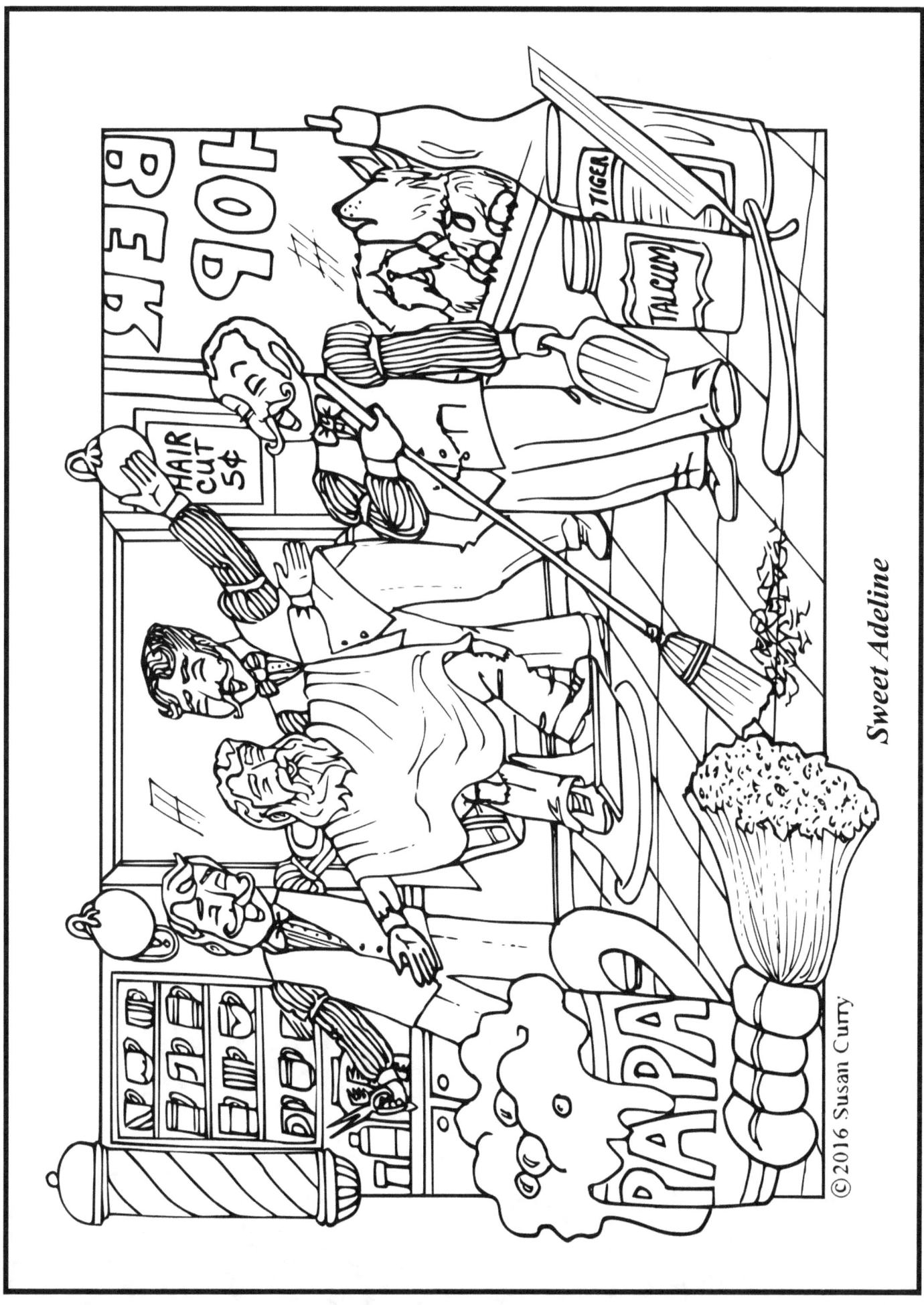

Sweet Adeline

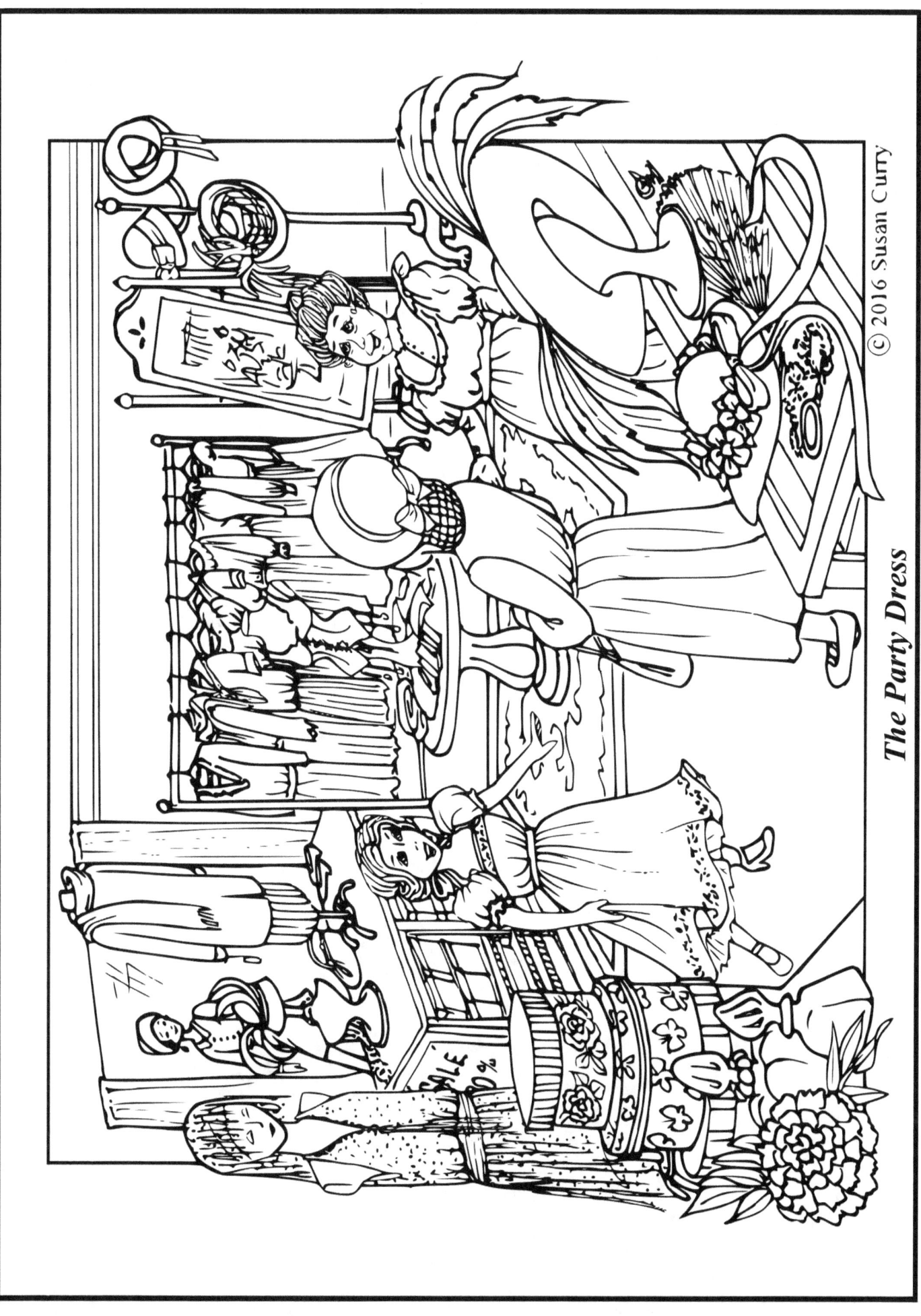

The Party Dress

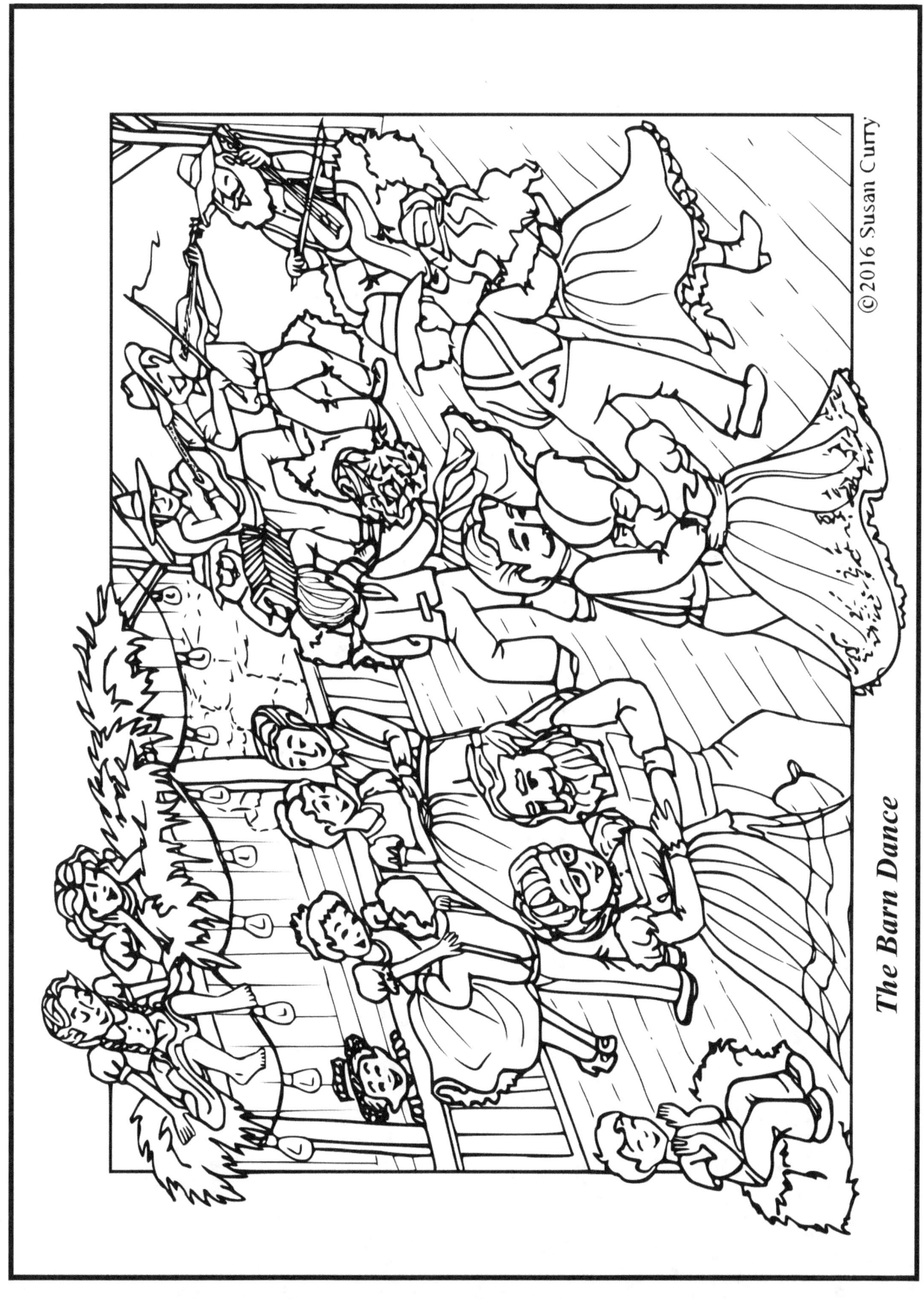

The Barn Dance

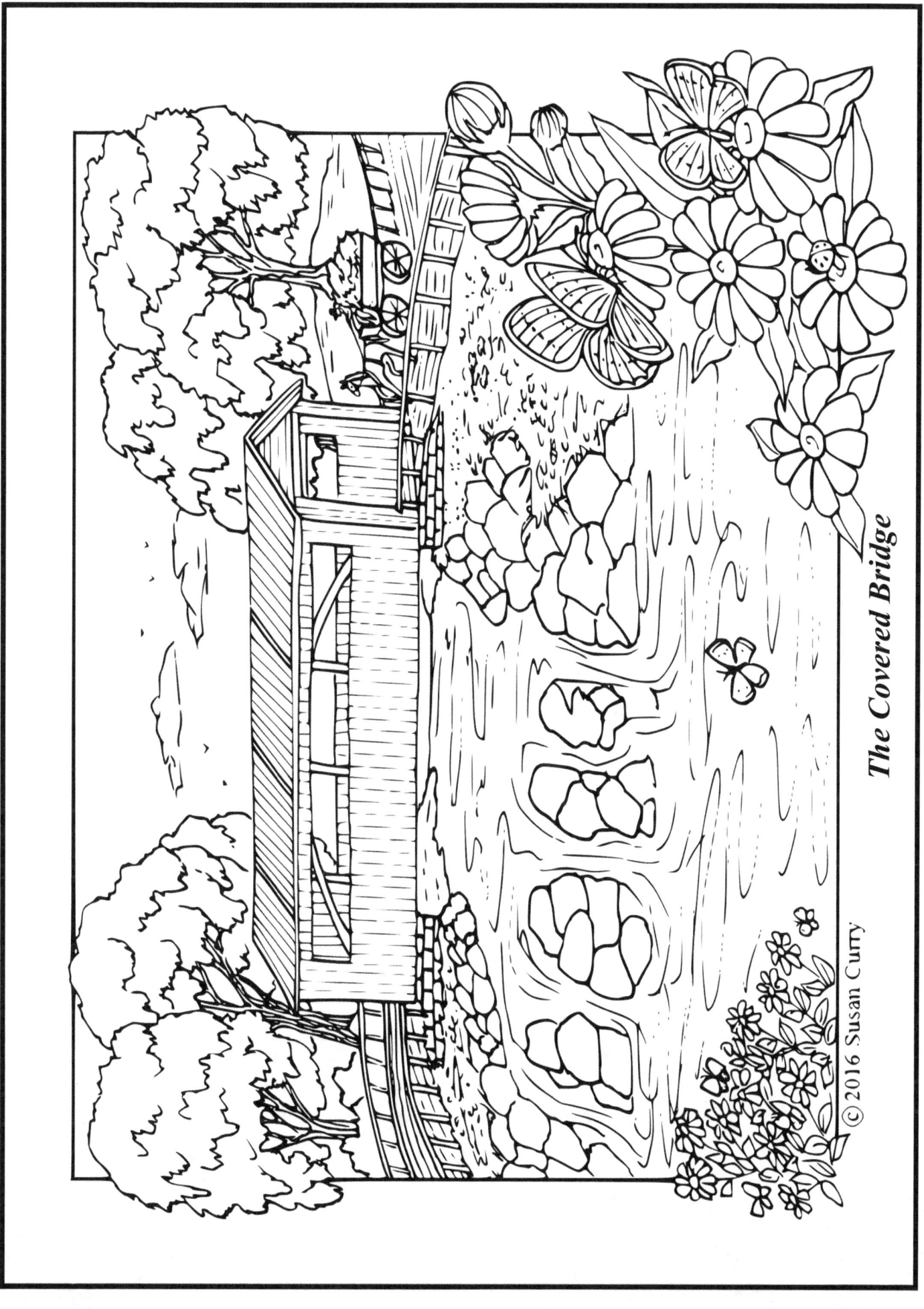

The Covered Bridge

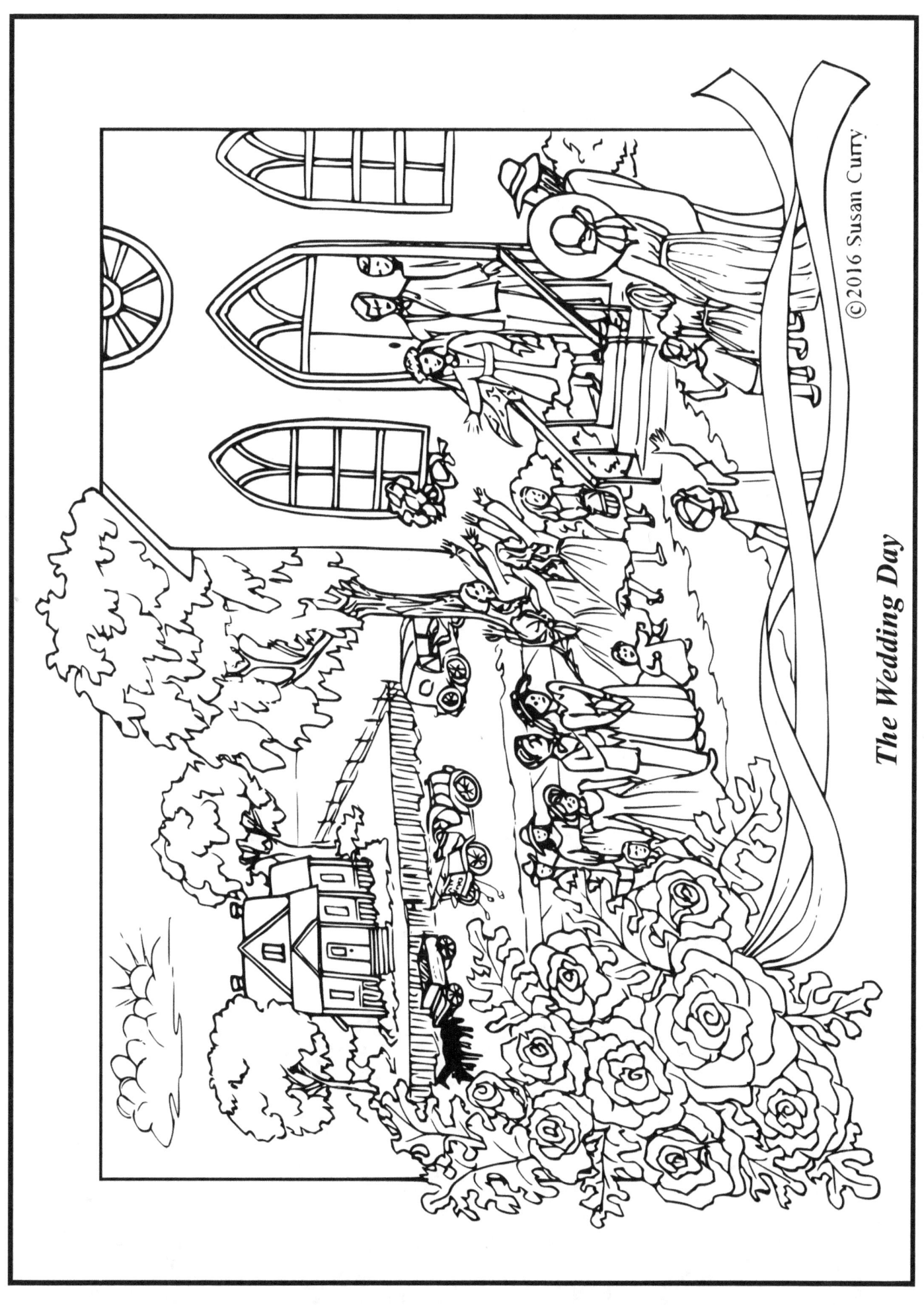

The Wedding Day

©2016 Susan Curry

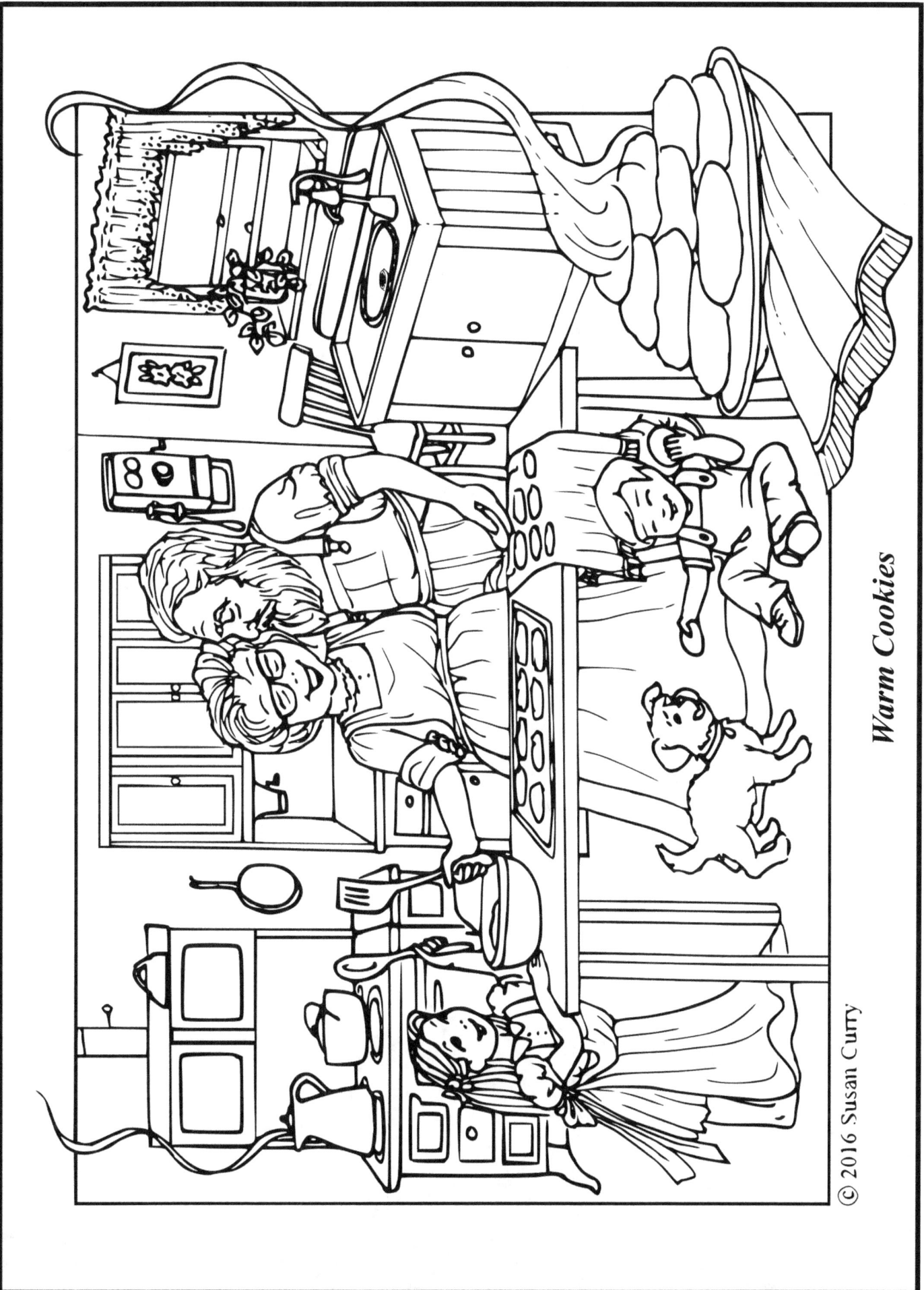

Warm Cookies

© 2016 Susan Curry

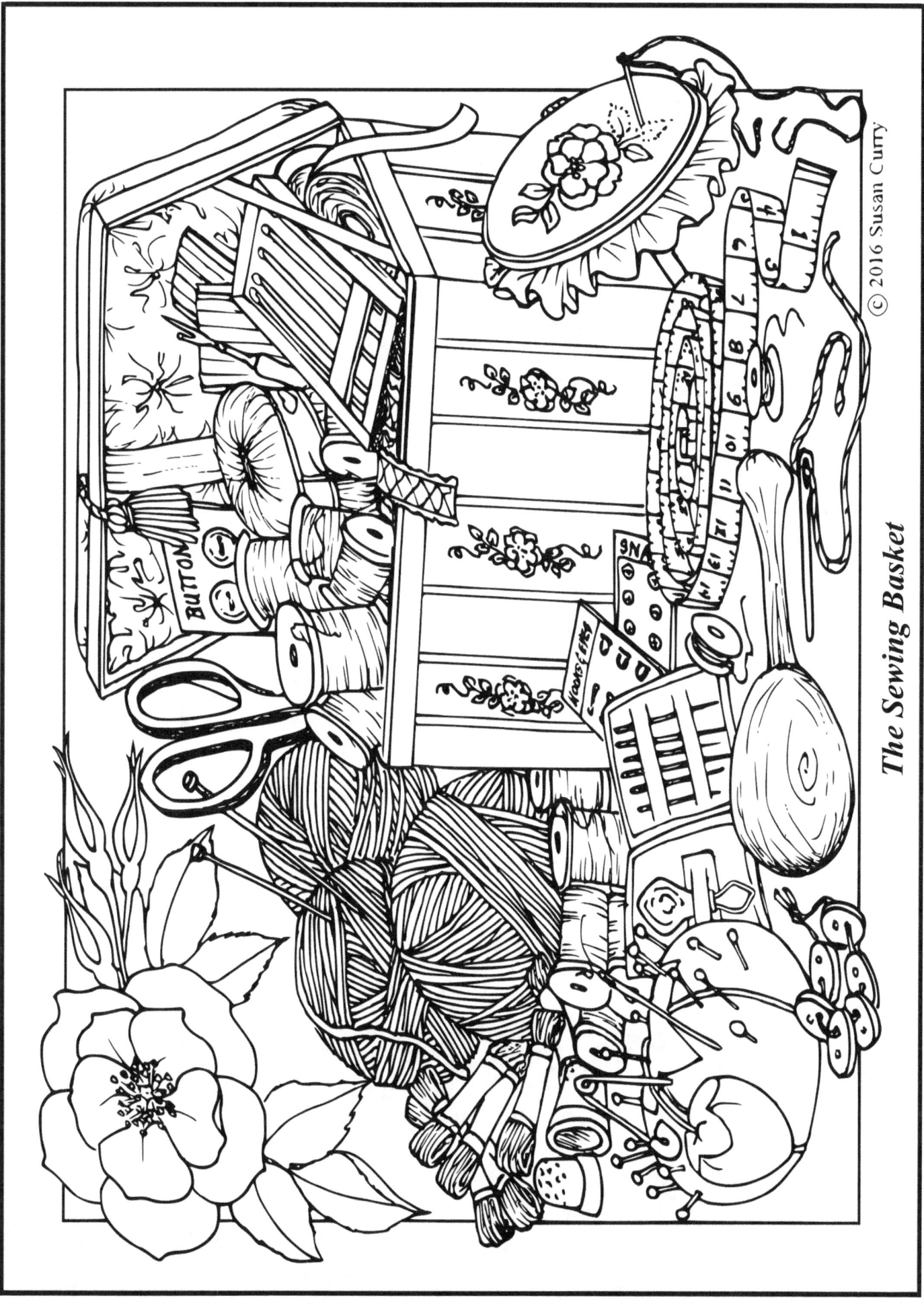

The Sewing Basket

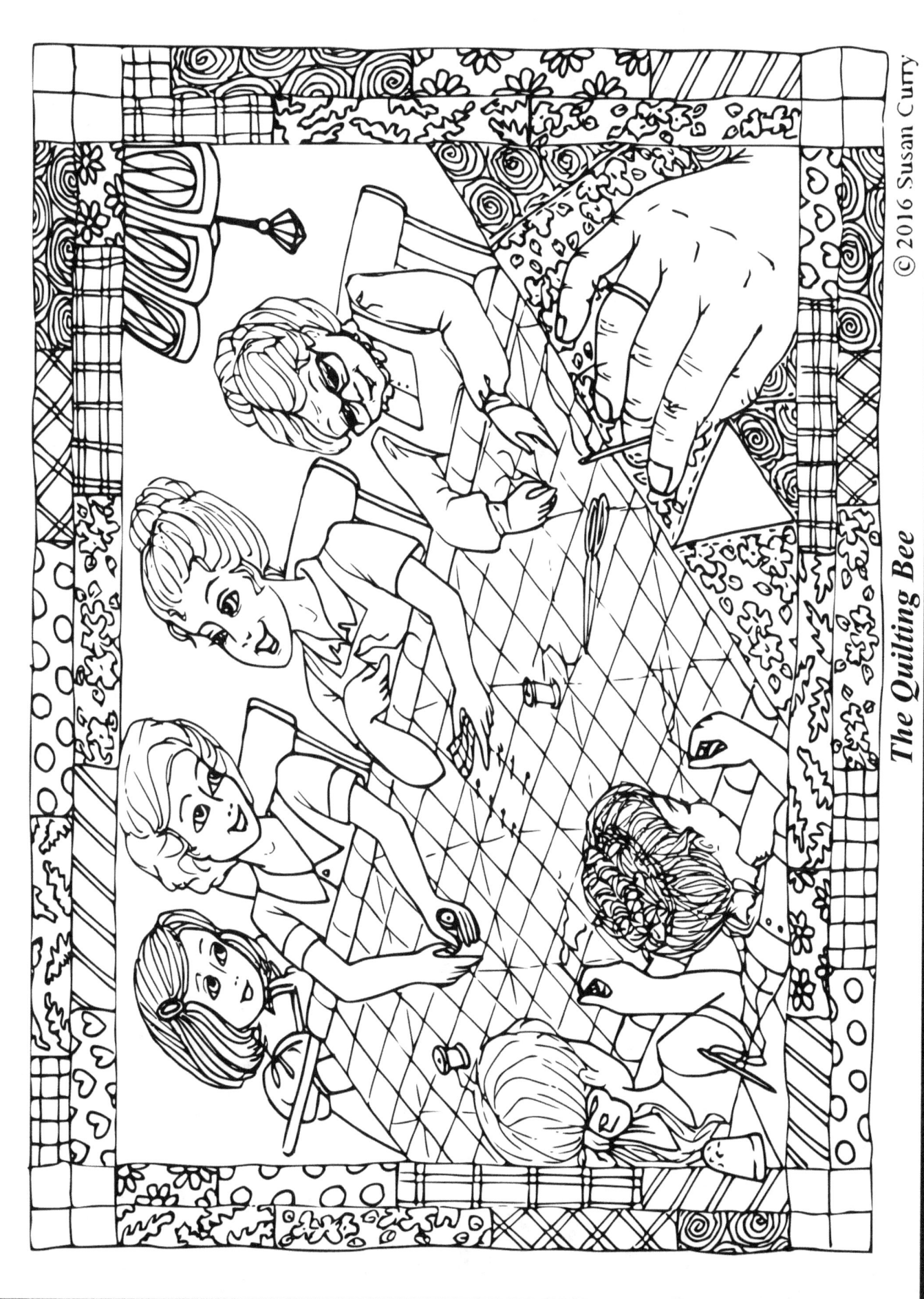

The Quilting Bee

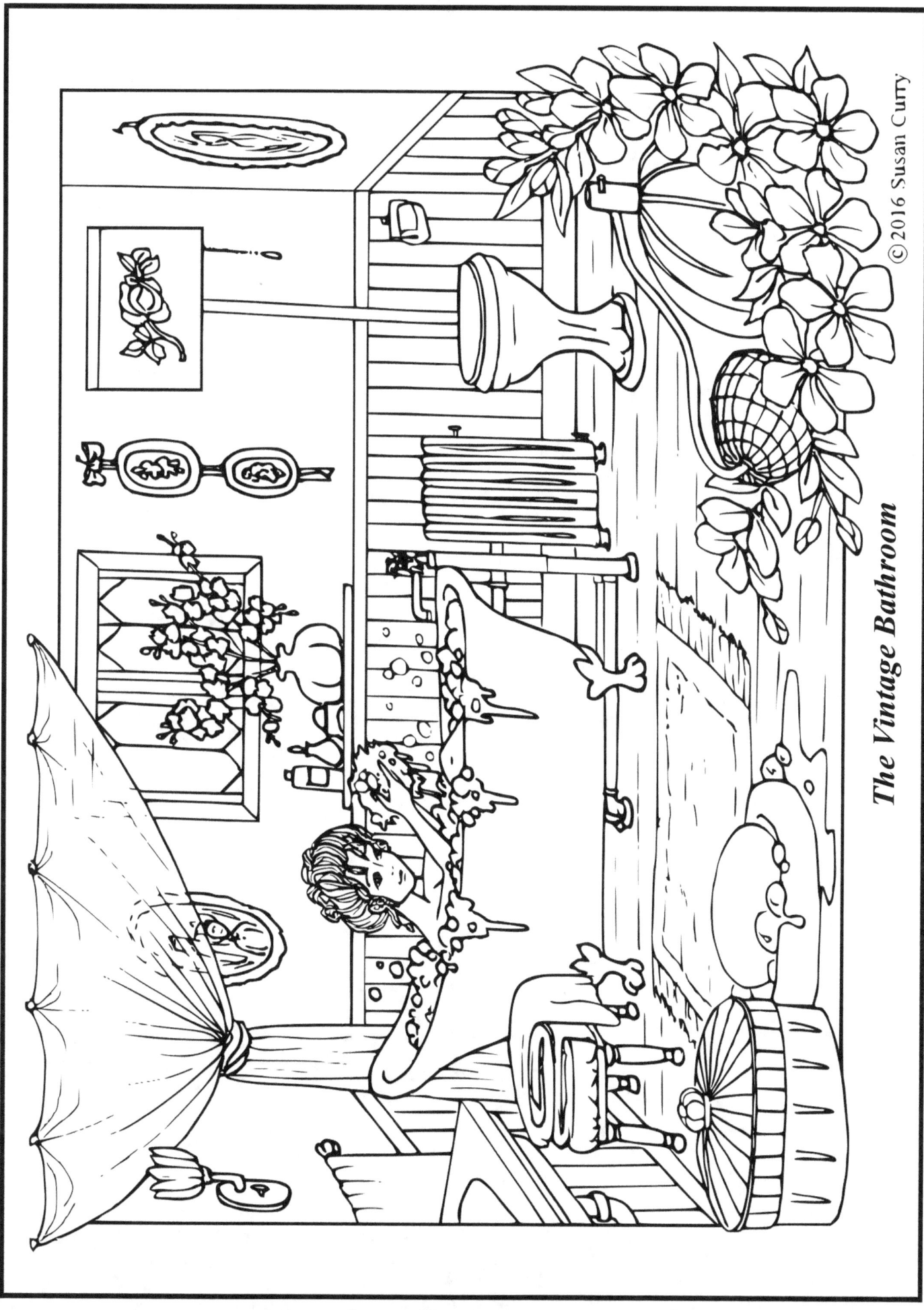

The Vintage Bathroom

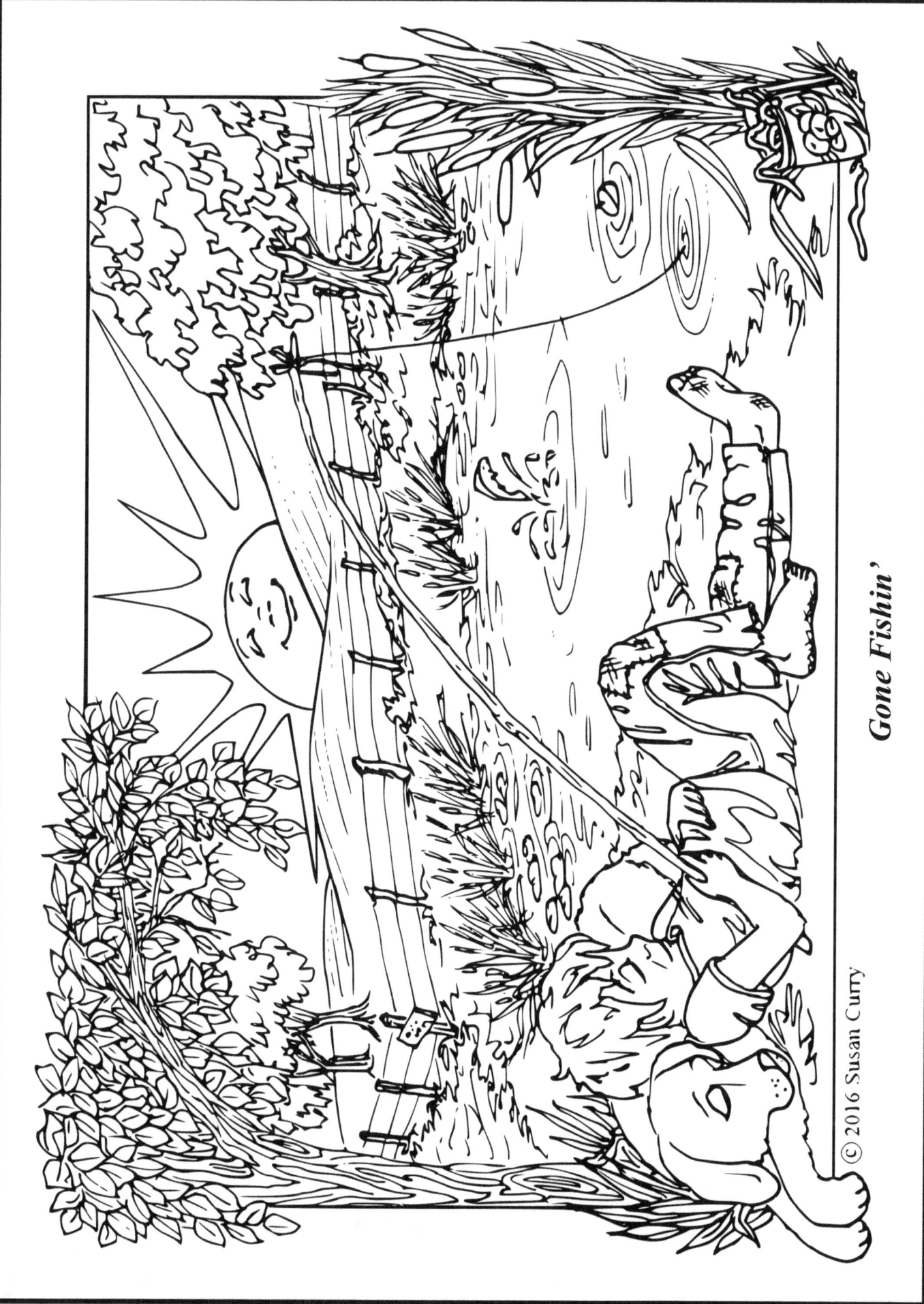

Gone Fishin'

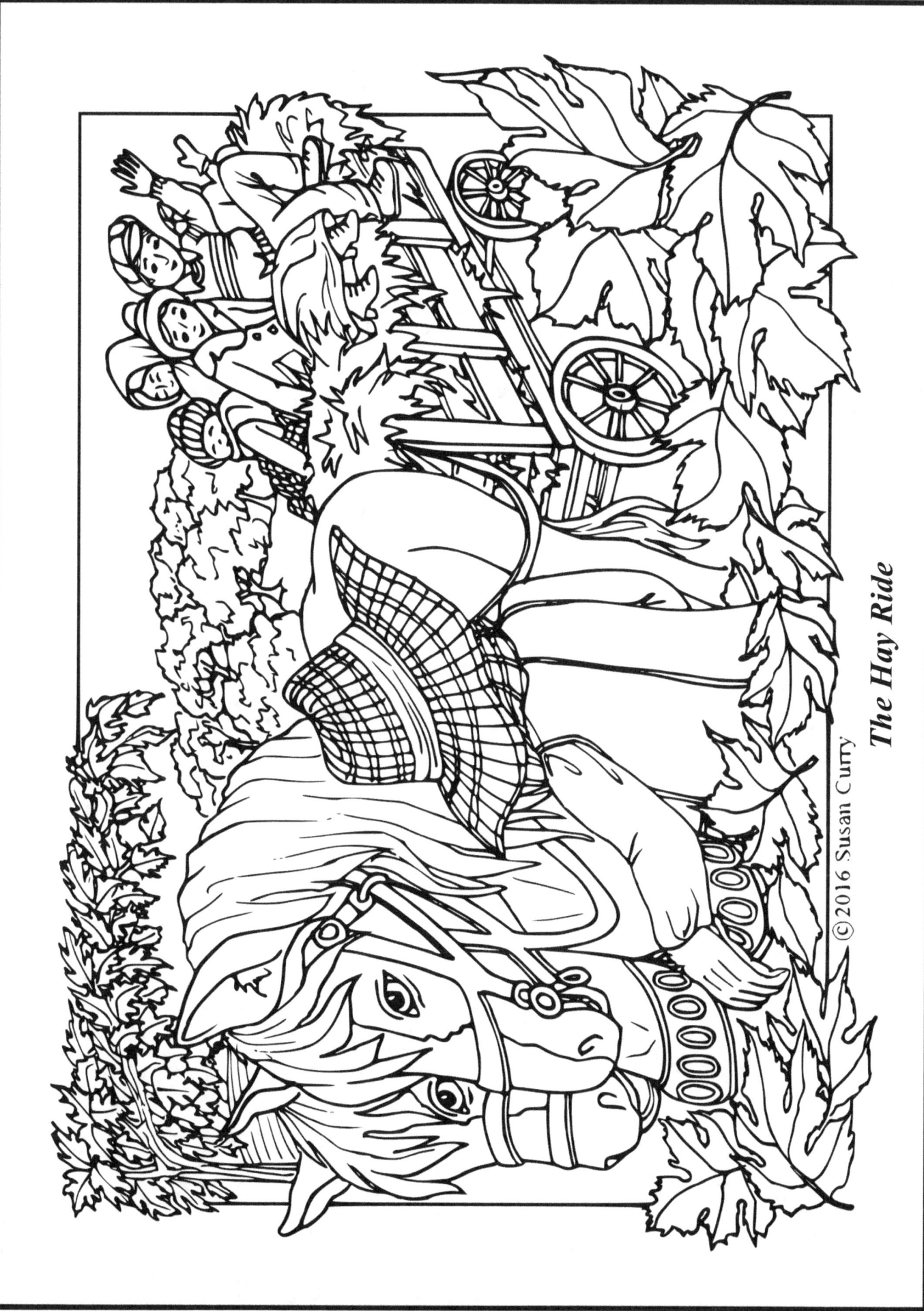

© 2016 Susan Curry

The Hay Ride

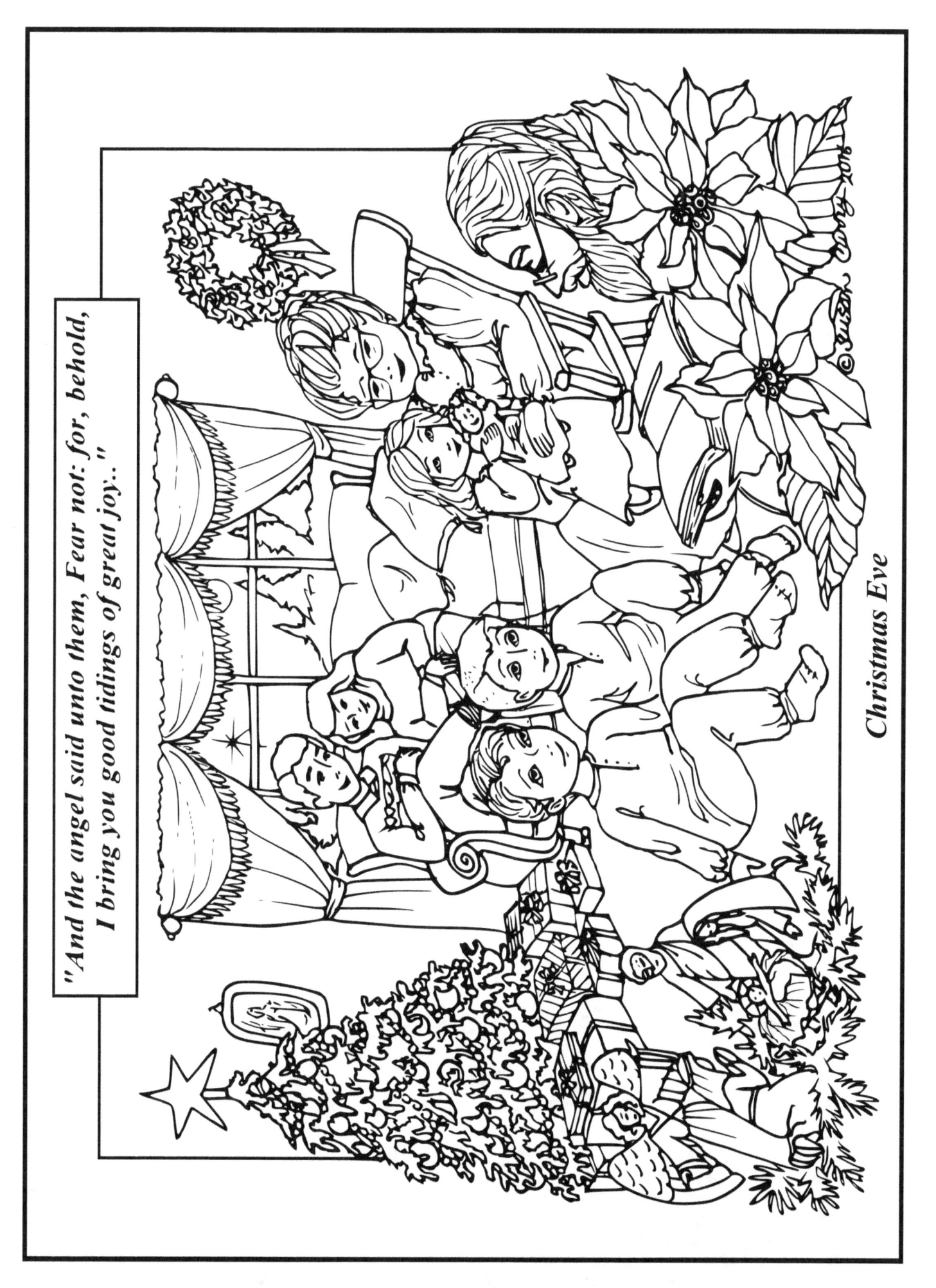

"And the angel said unto them, Fear not: for, behold, I bring you good tidings of great joy..."

Christmas Eve

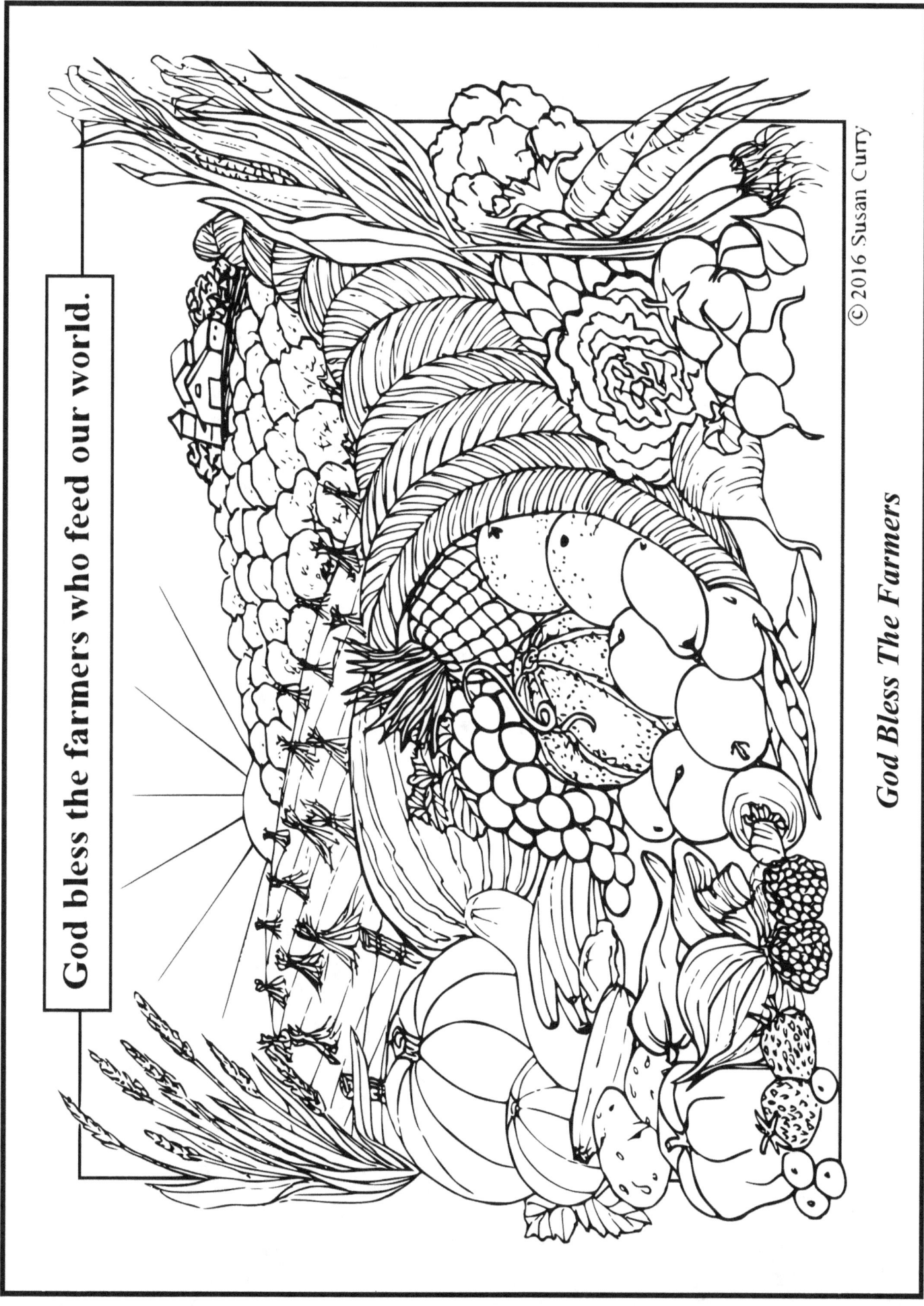

God bless the farmers who feed our world.

God Bless The Farmers

© 2016 Susan Curry

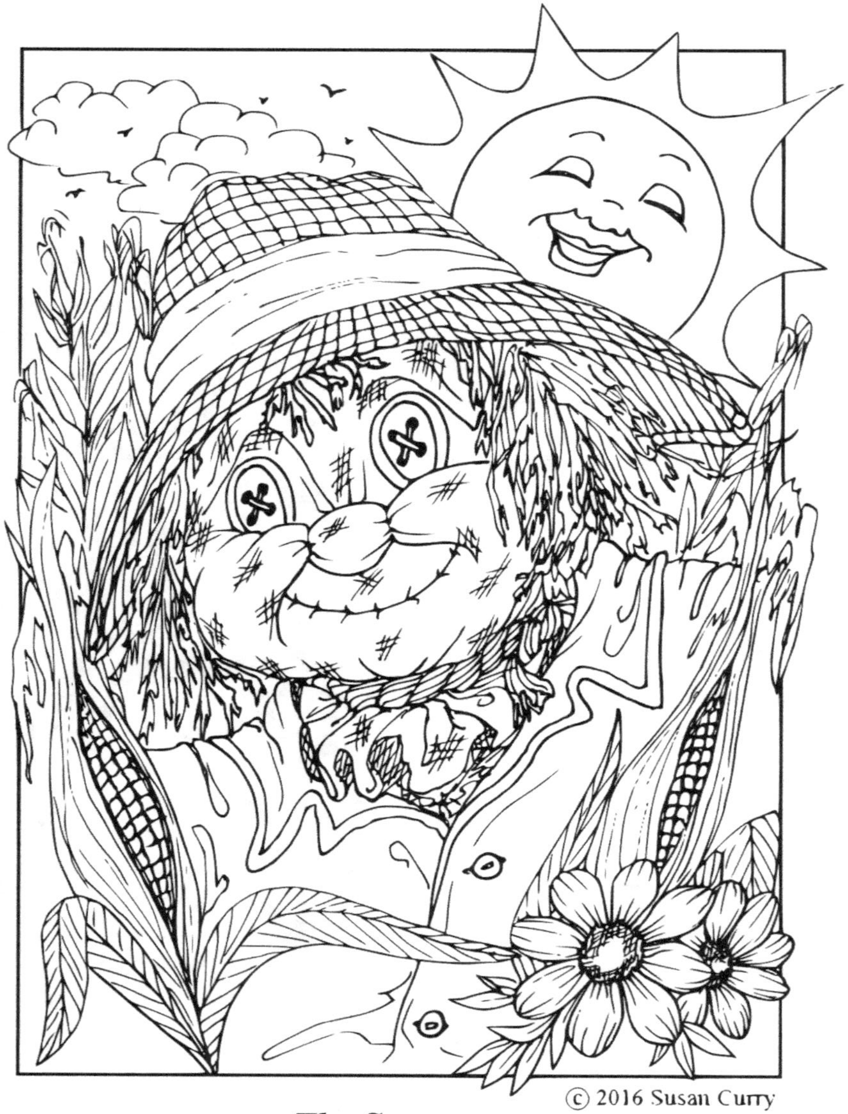

The Outhouse

© 2016 Susan Curry

The Scarecrow

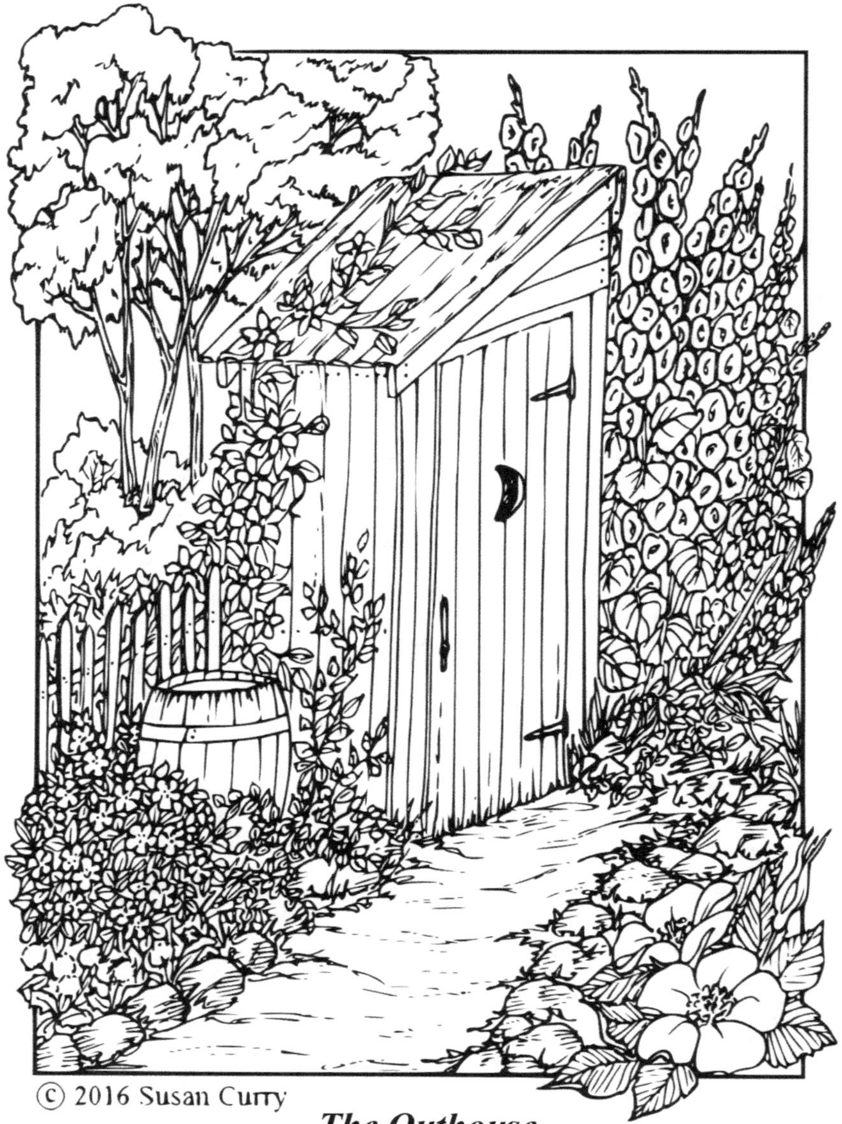

© 2016 Susan Curry

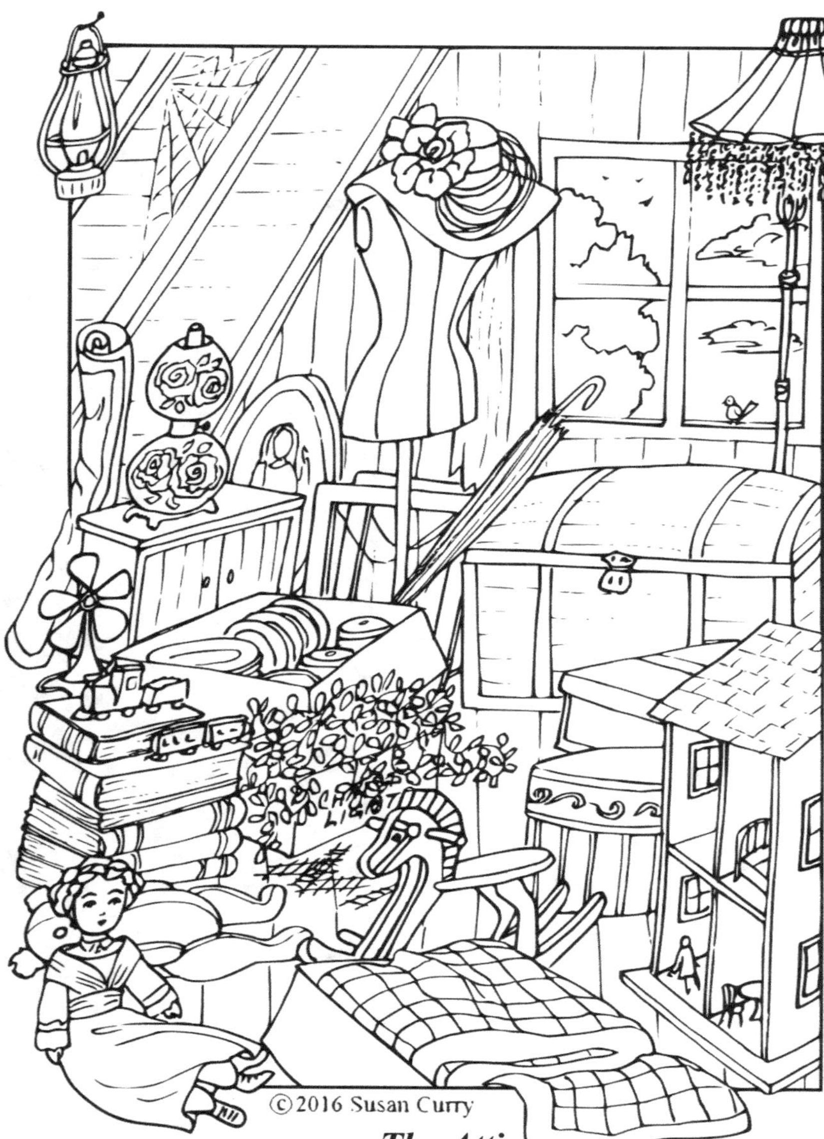

Nana's Flower Garden

© 2016 Susan Curry

© 2016 Susan Curry

The Attic

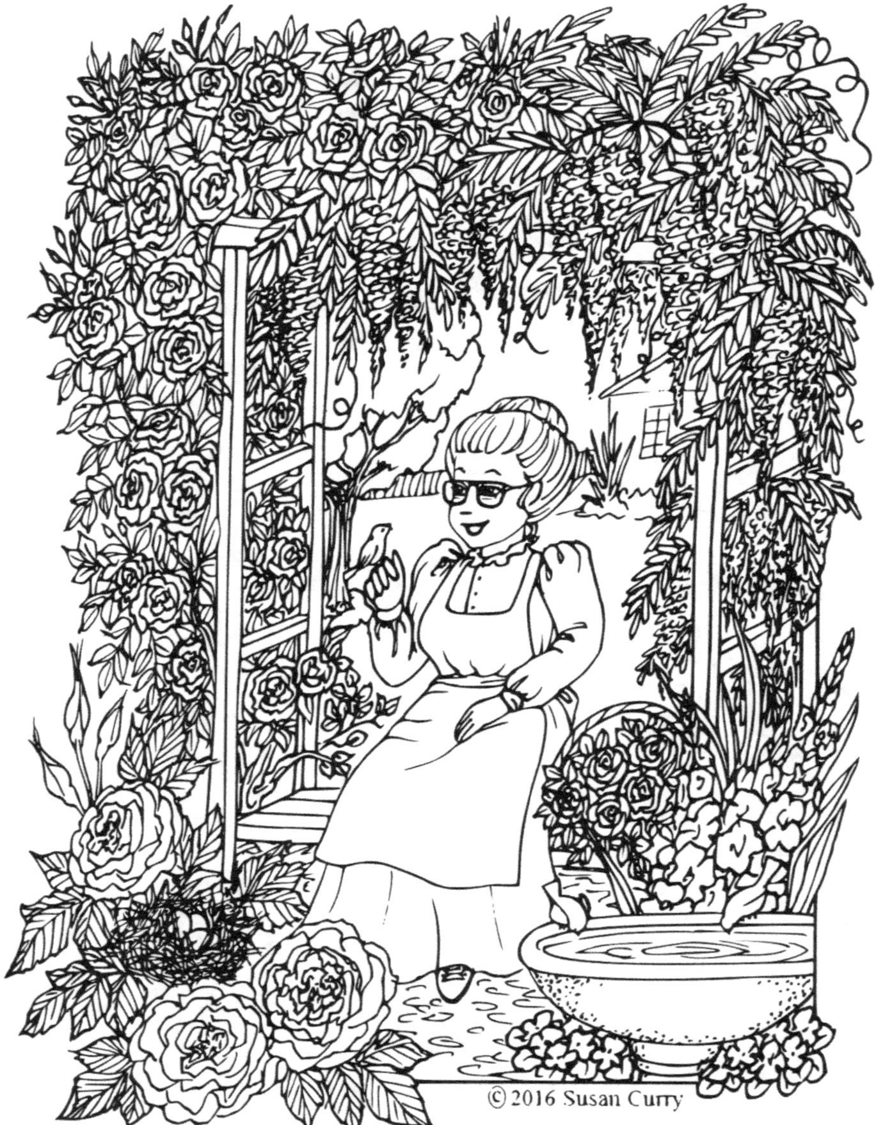

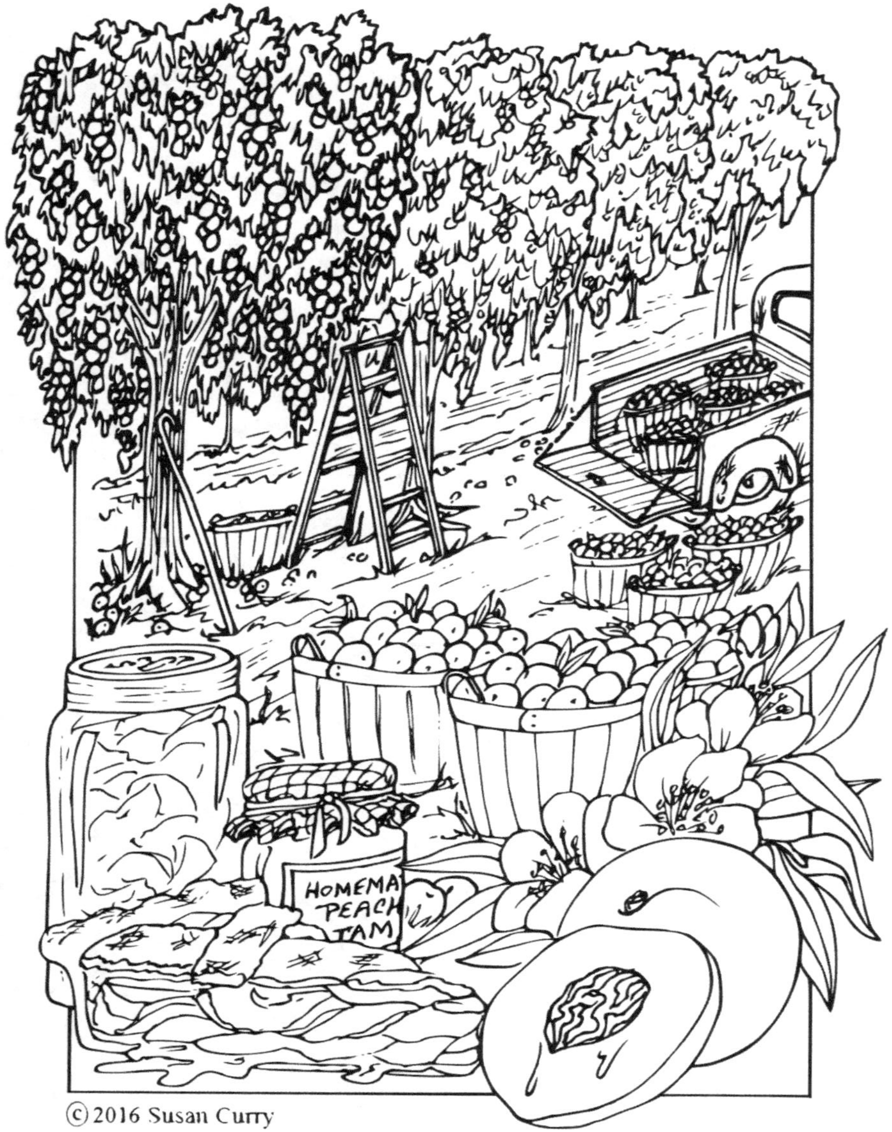

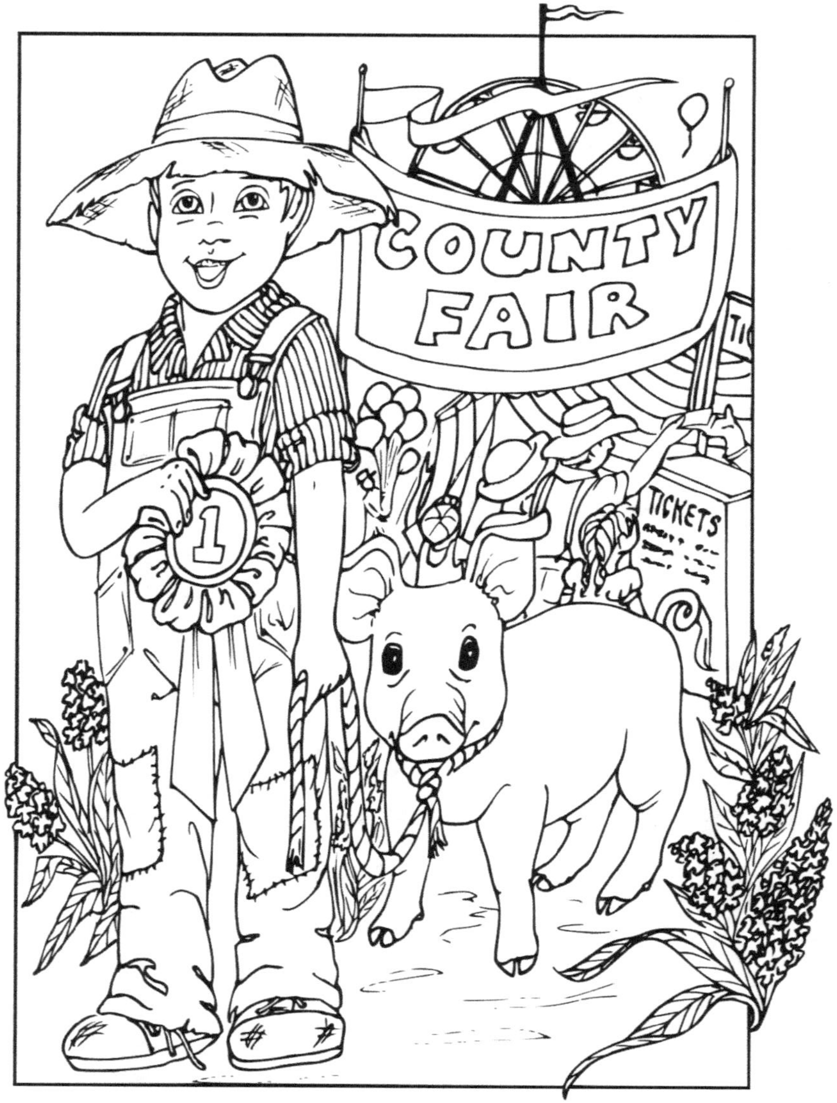

The Prize Winning Pig

© 2016 Susan Curry   *The Peach Harvest*

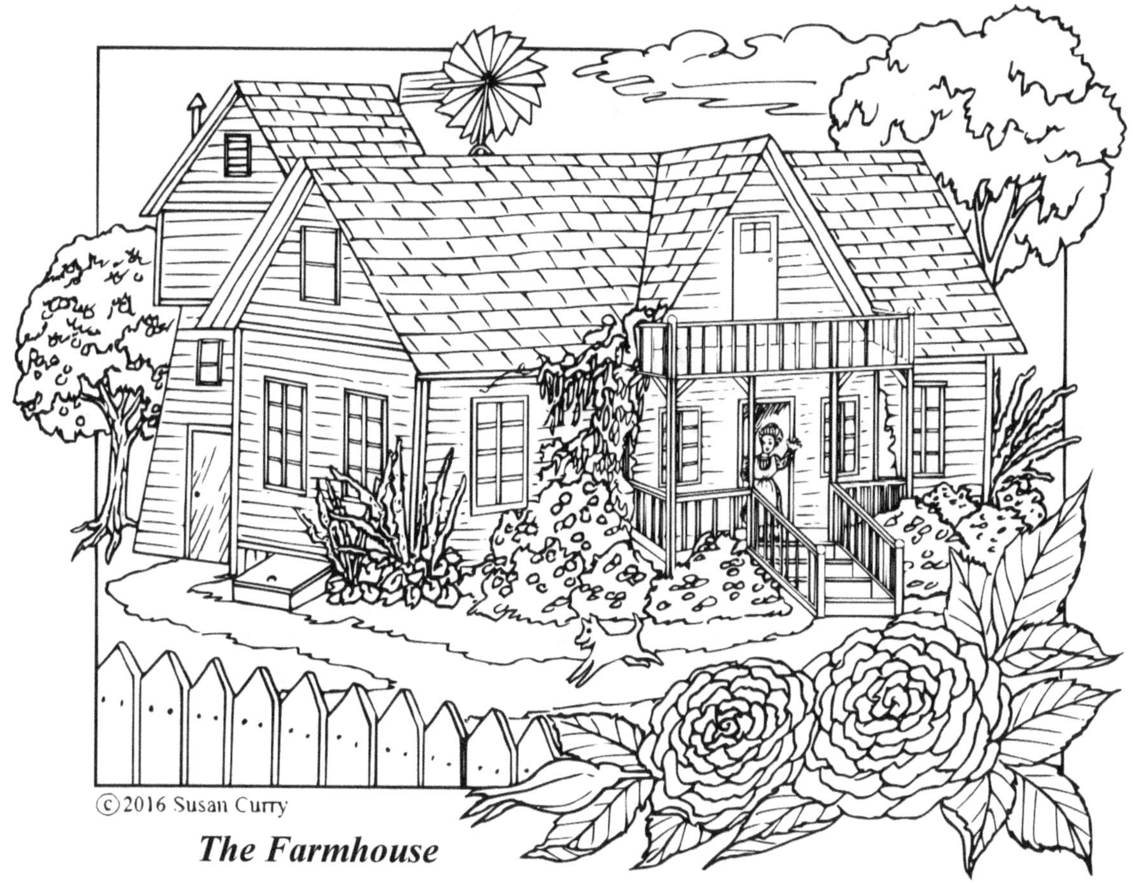

The Farmhouse

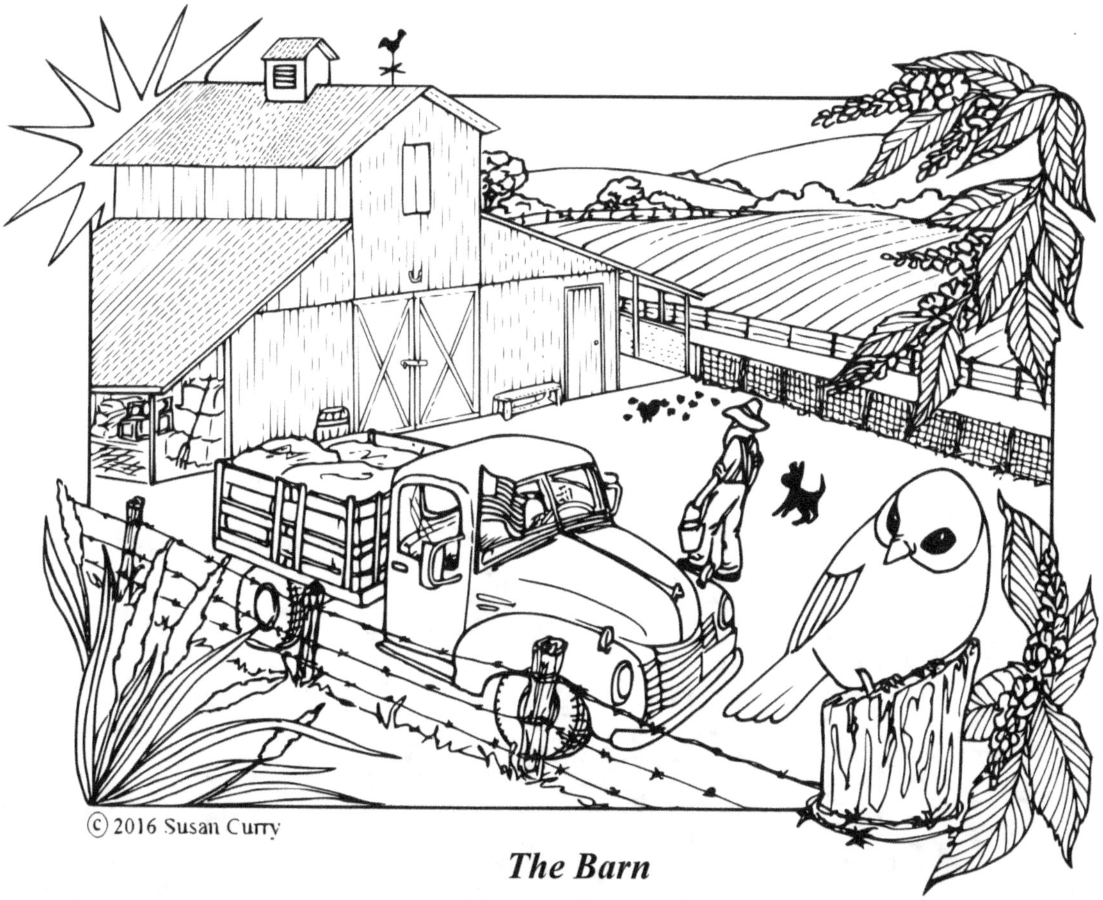

The Barn

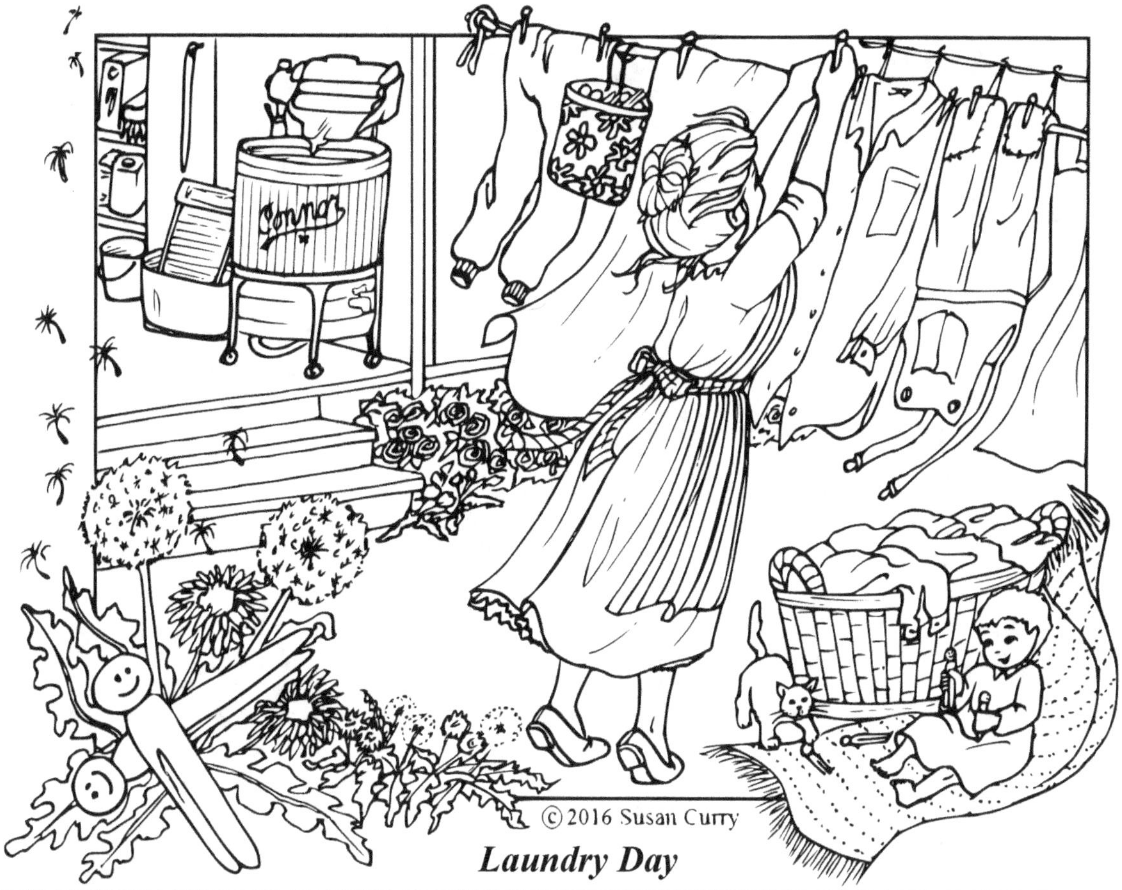

© 2016 Susan Curry

Laundry Day

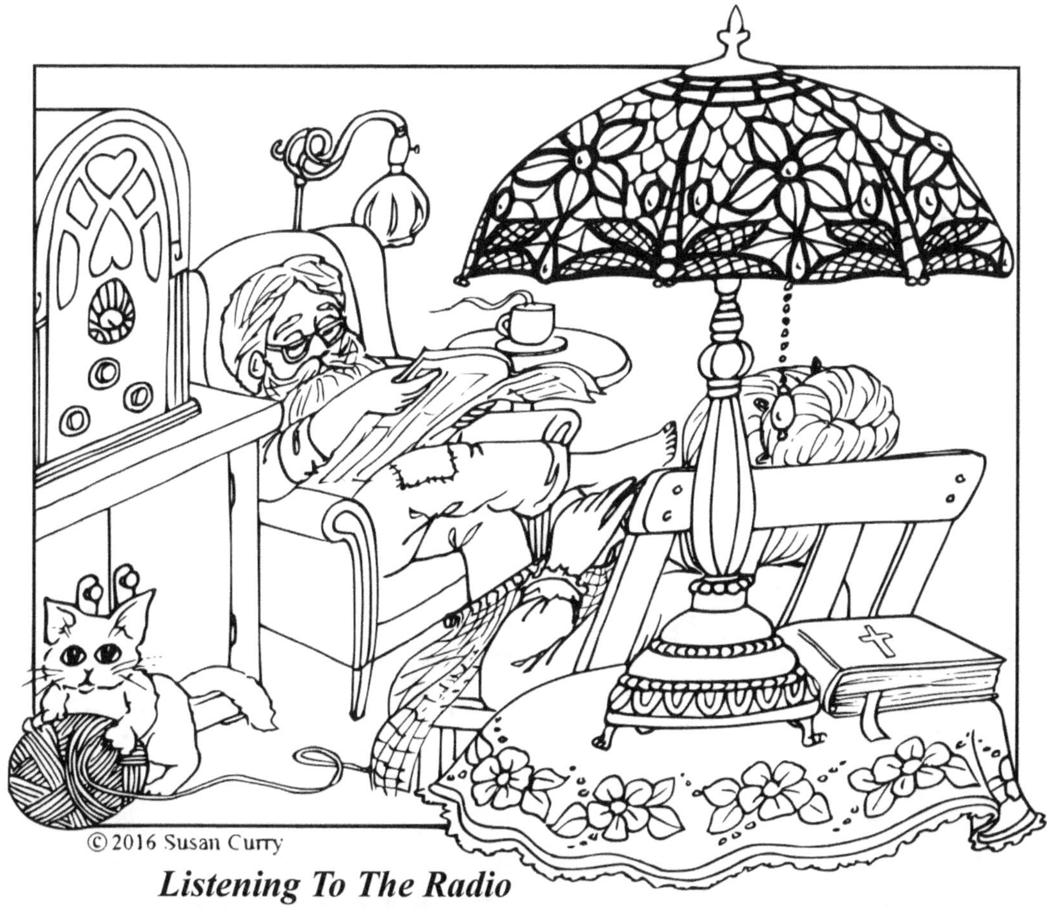

© 2016 Susan Curry

Listening To The Radio

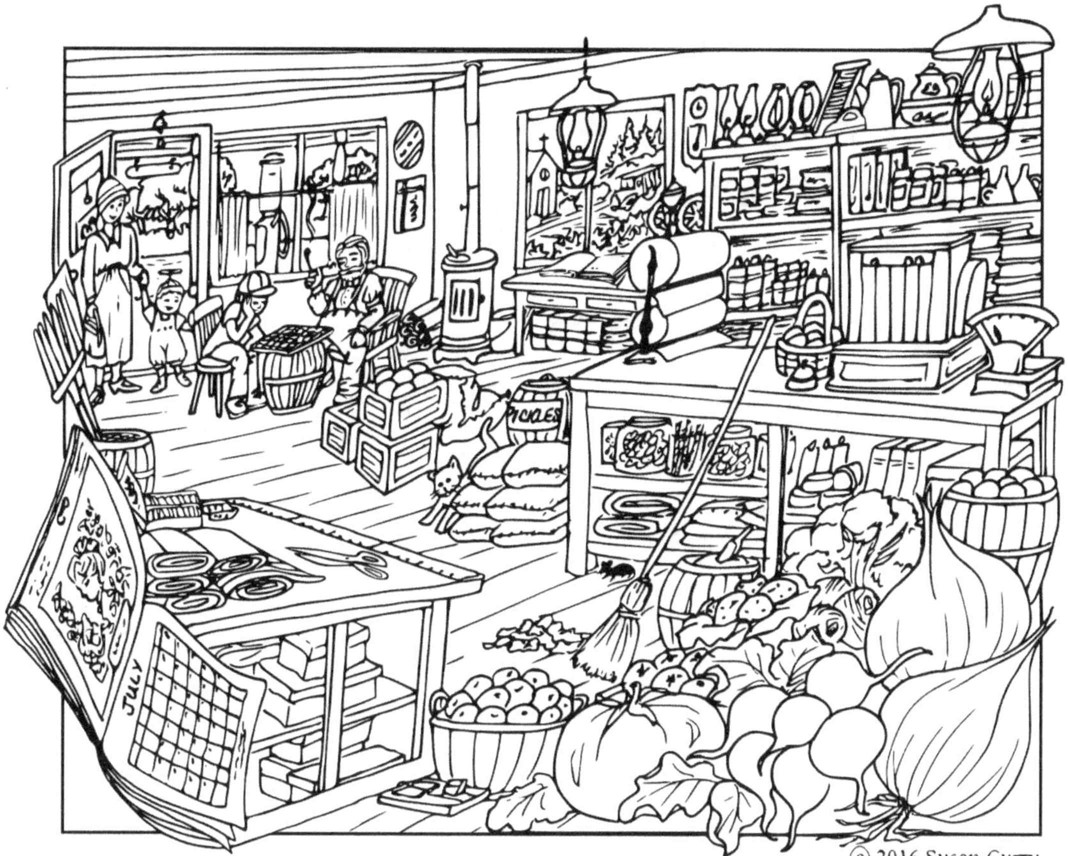

The General Store

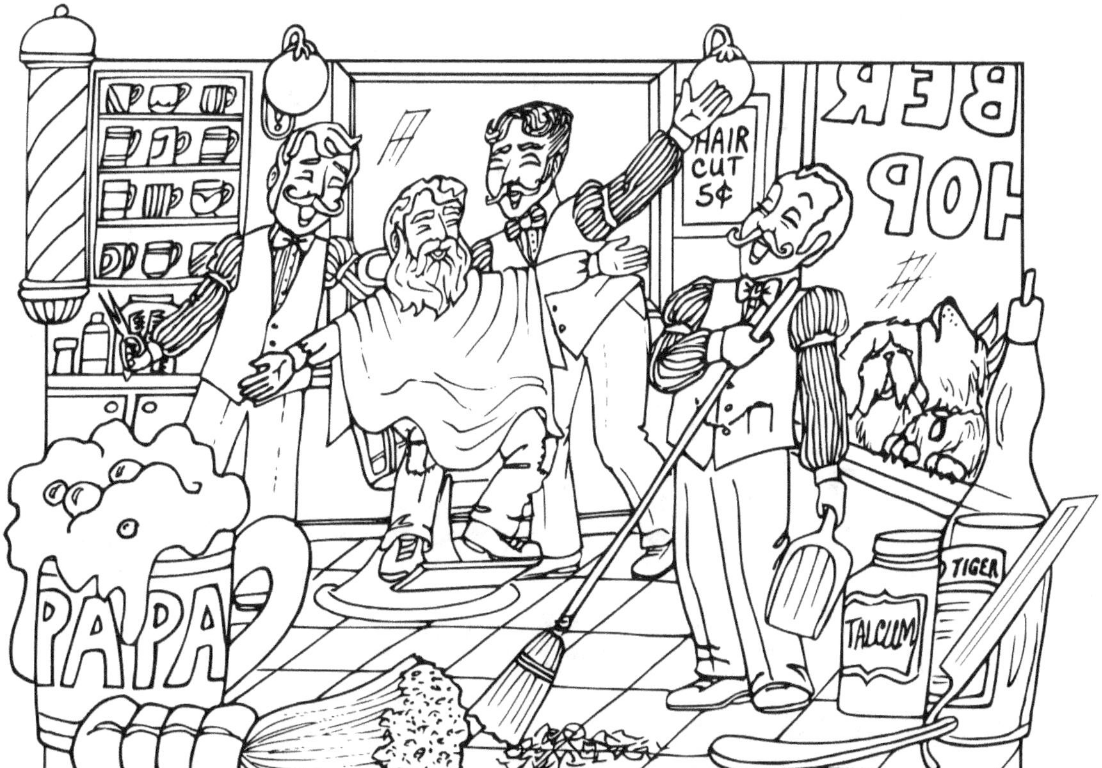

© 2016 Susan Curry

Sweet Adeline

© 2016 Susan Curry

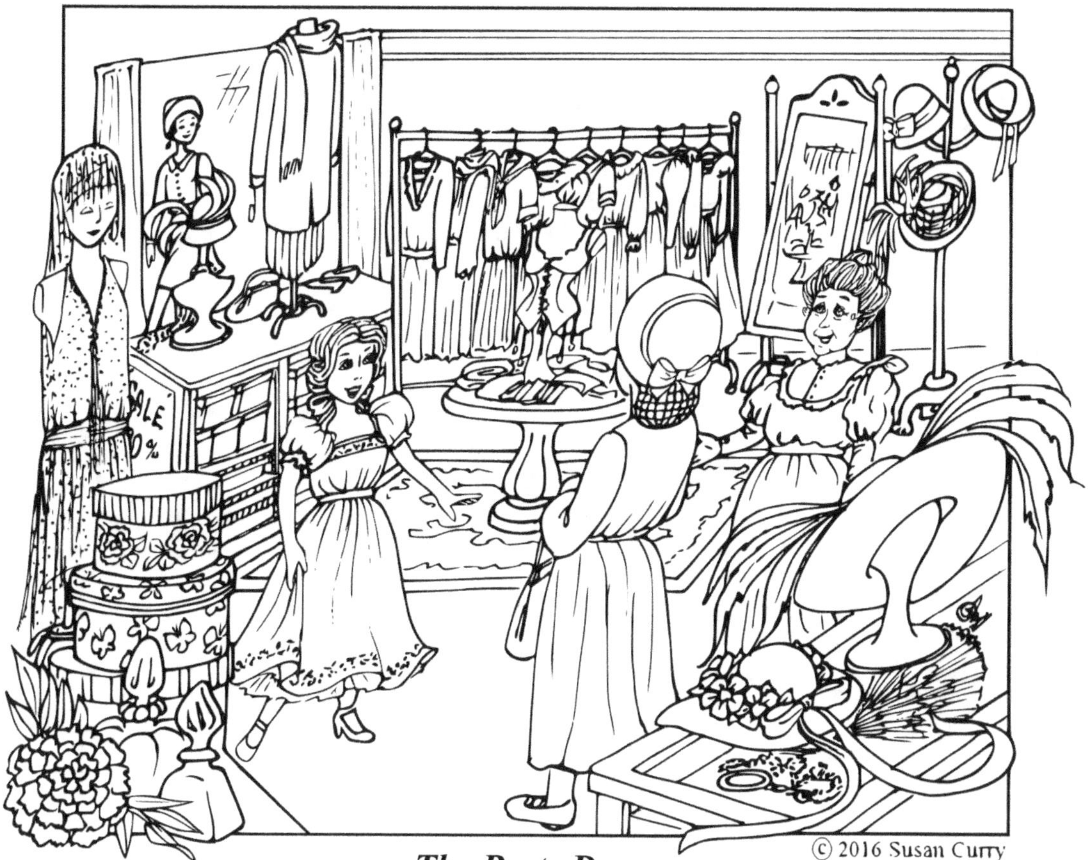

The Party Dress

© 2016 Susan Curry

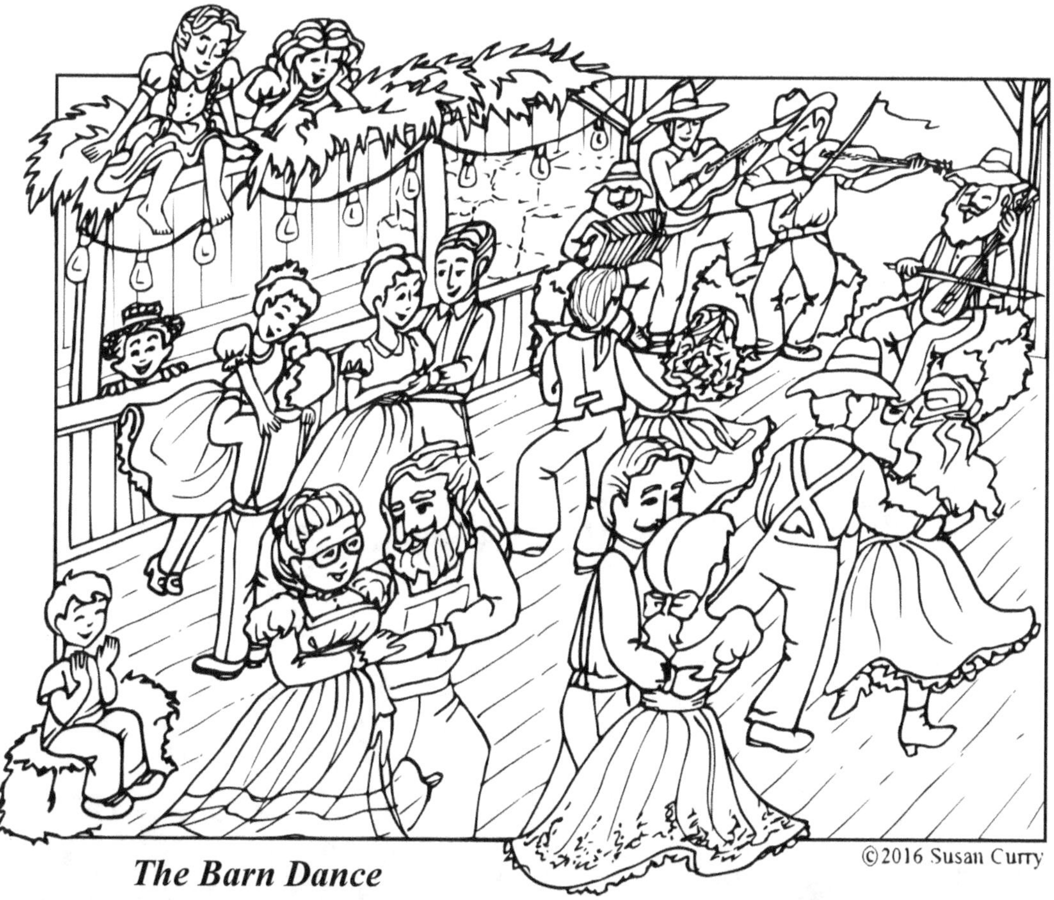

The Barn Dance

©2016 Susan Curry

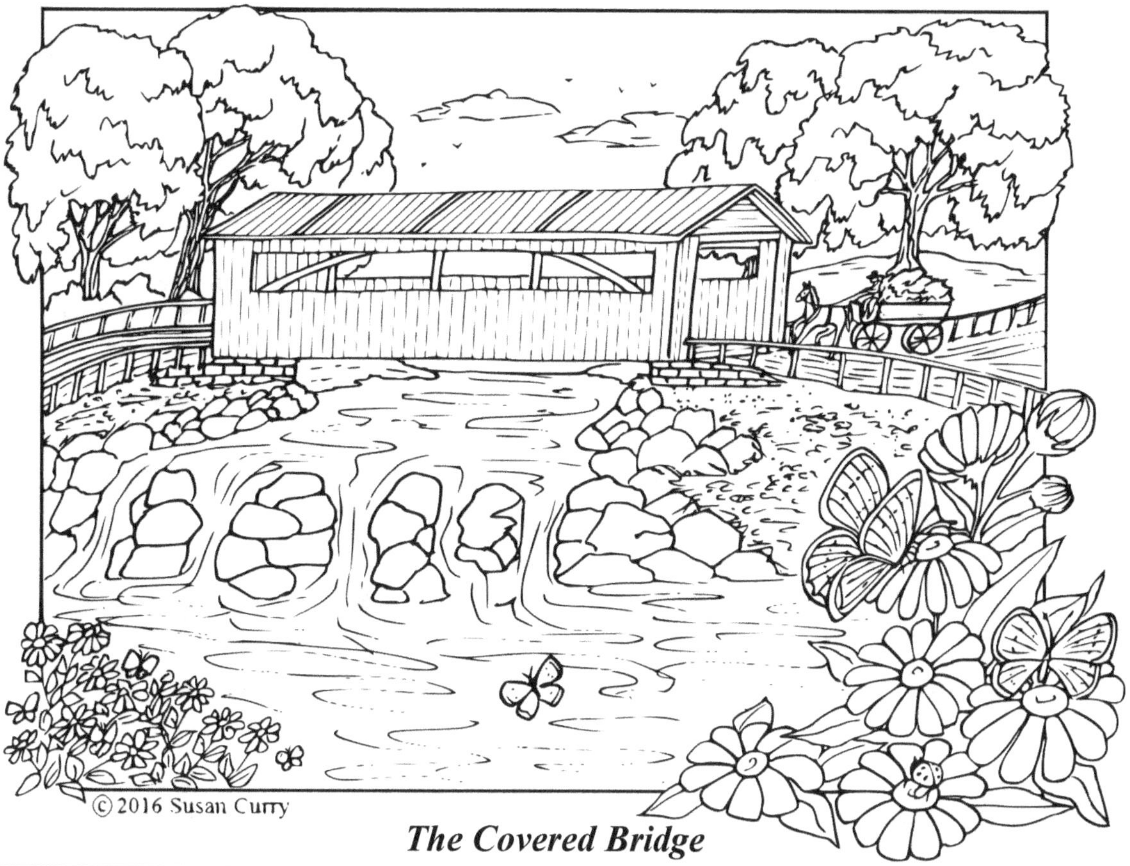

The Covered Bridge

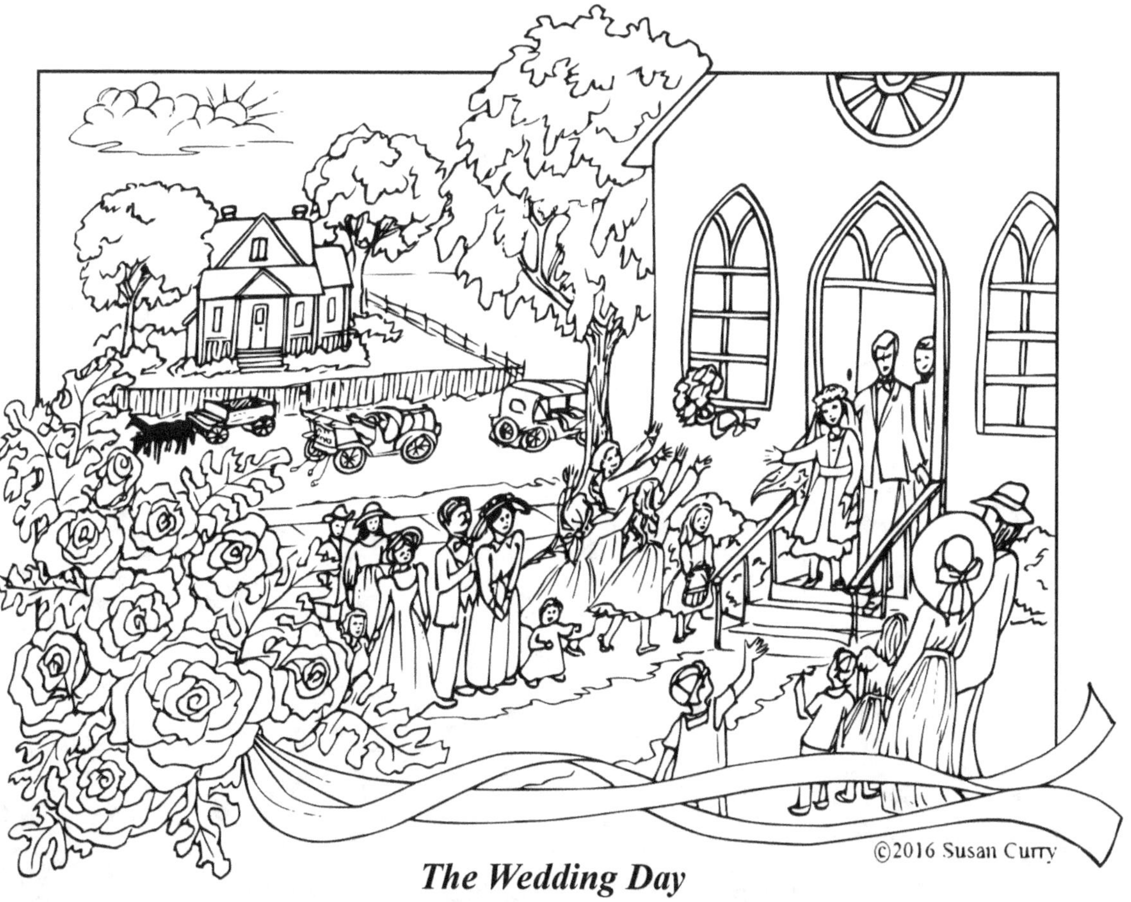

© 2016 Susan Curry

The Wedding Day

©2016 Susan Curry

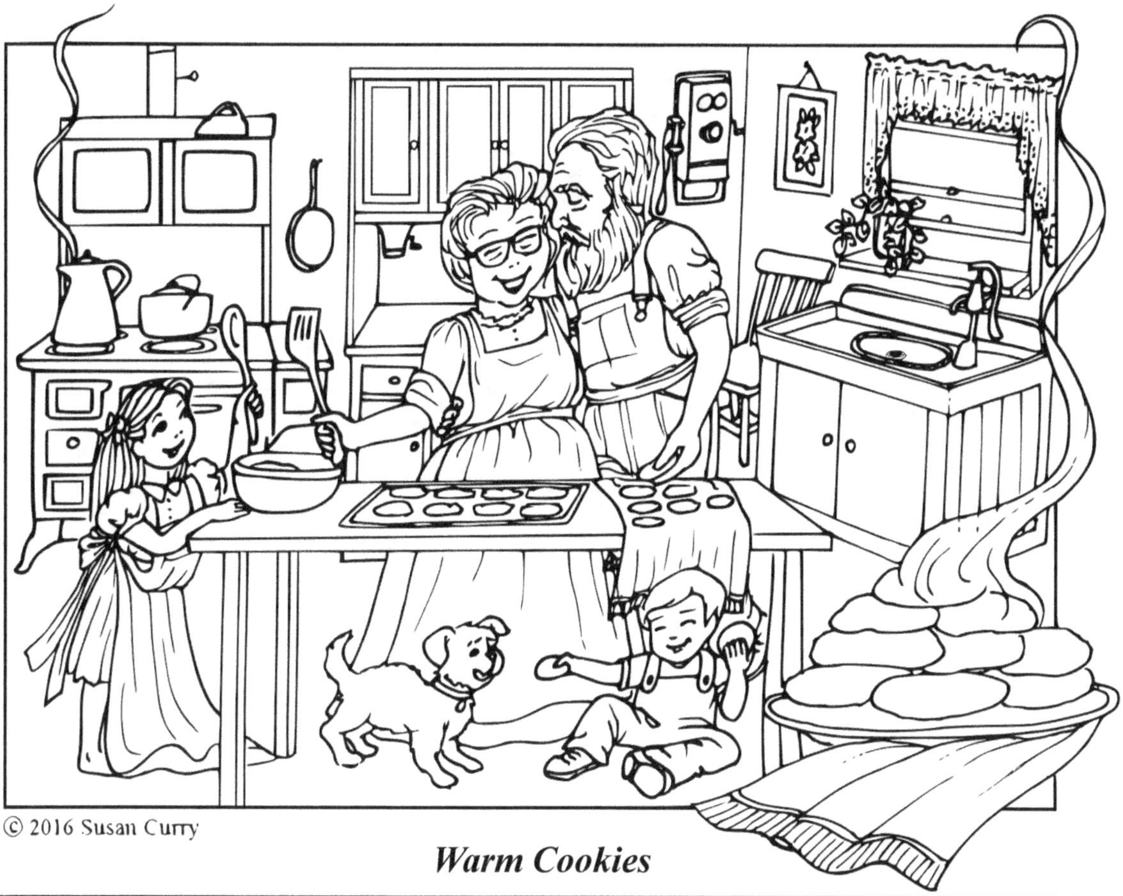

Warm Cookies

© 2016 Susan Curry

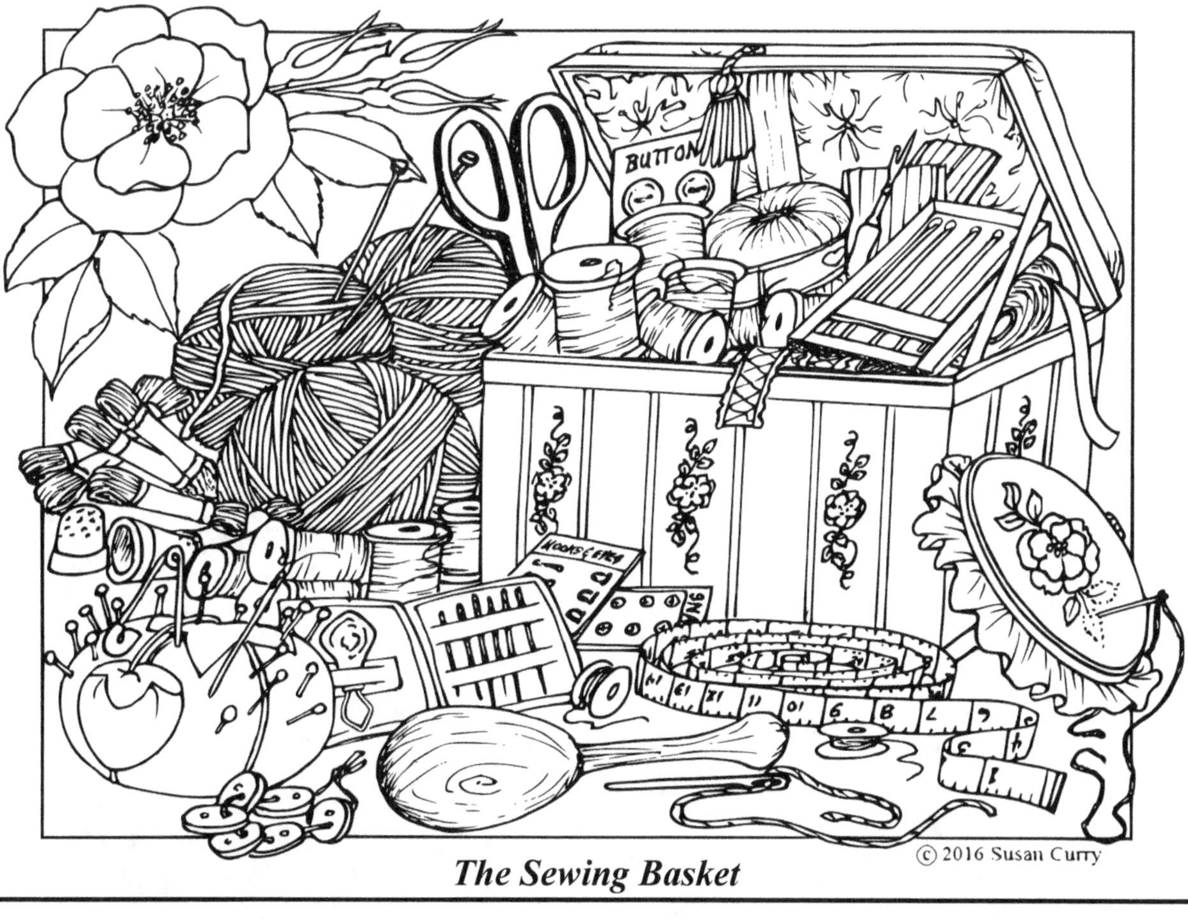

The Sewing Basket

© 2016 Susan Curry

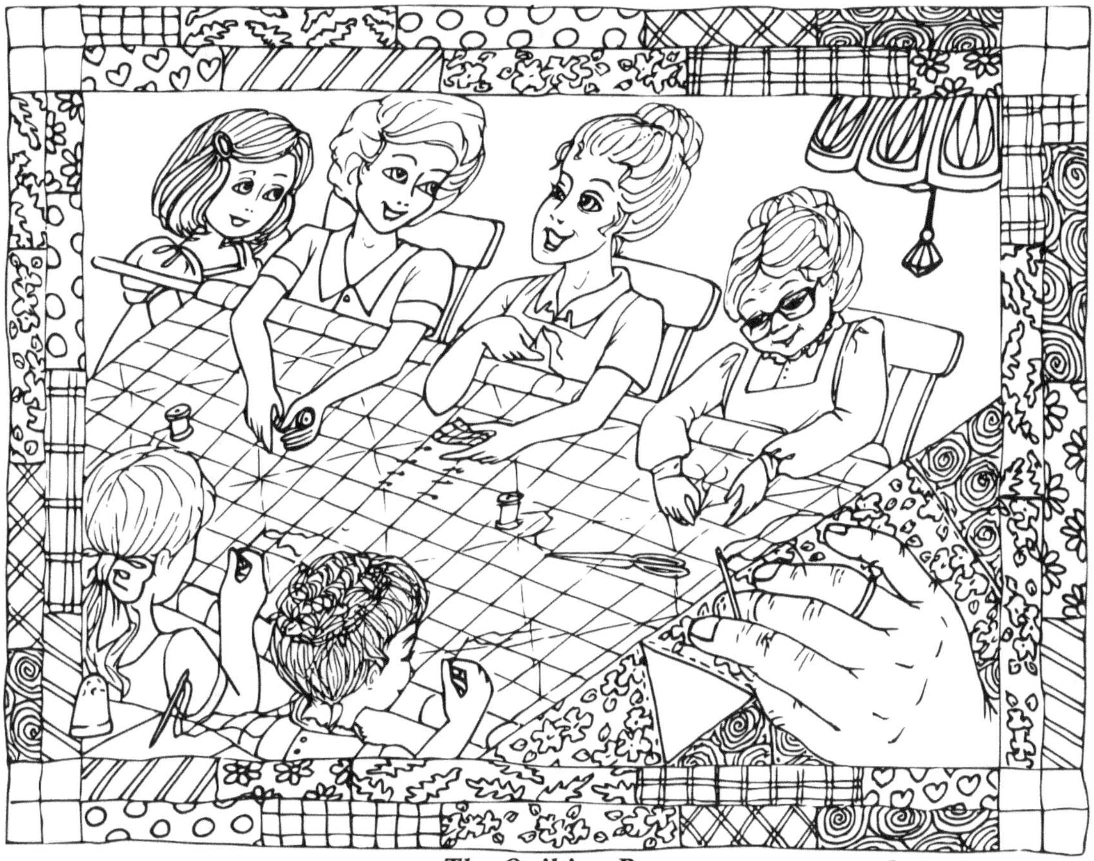

The Quilting Bee © 2016 Susan Curry

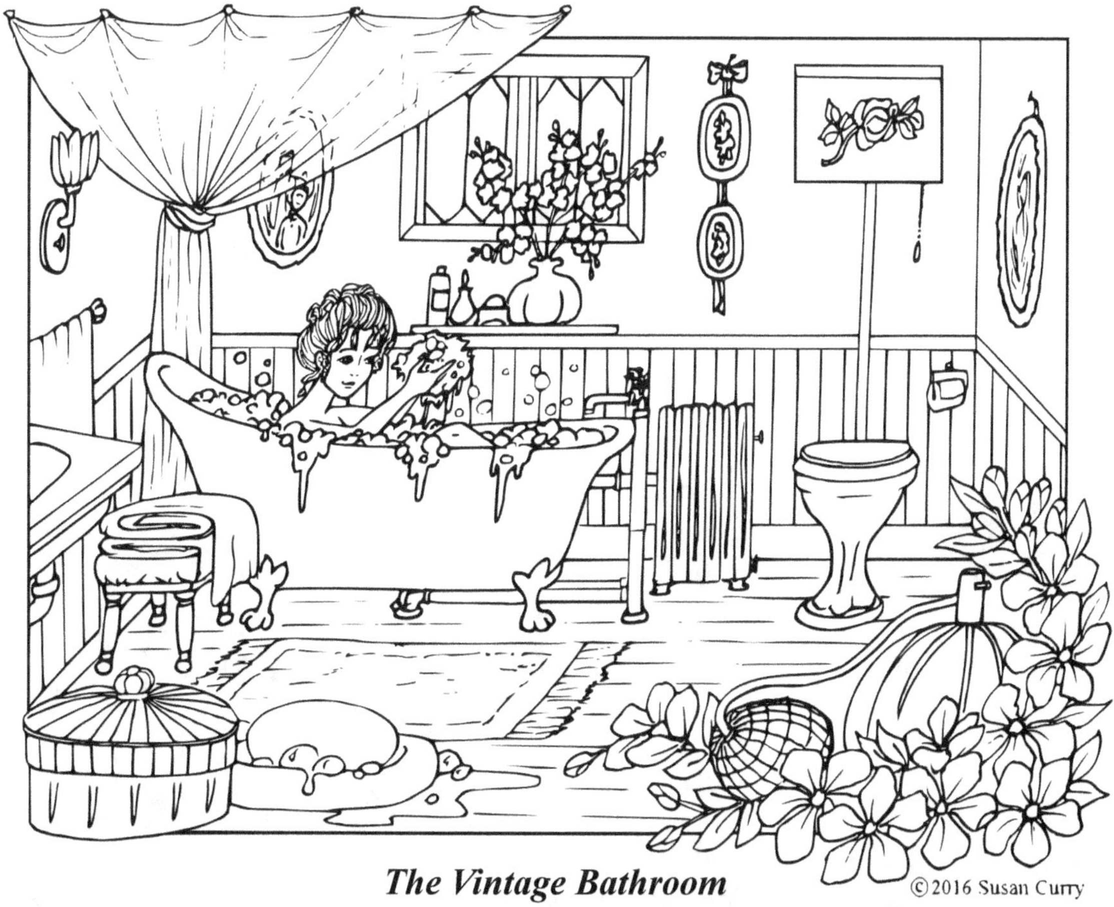

The Vintage Bathroom © 2016 Susan Curry

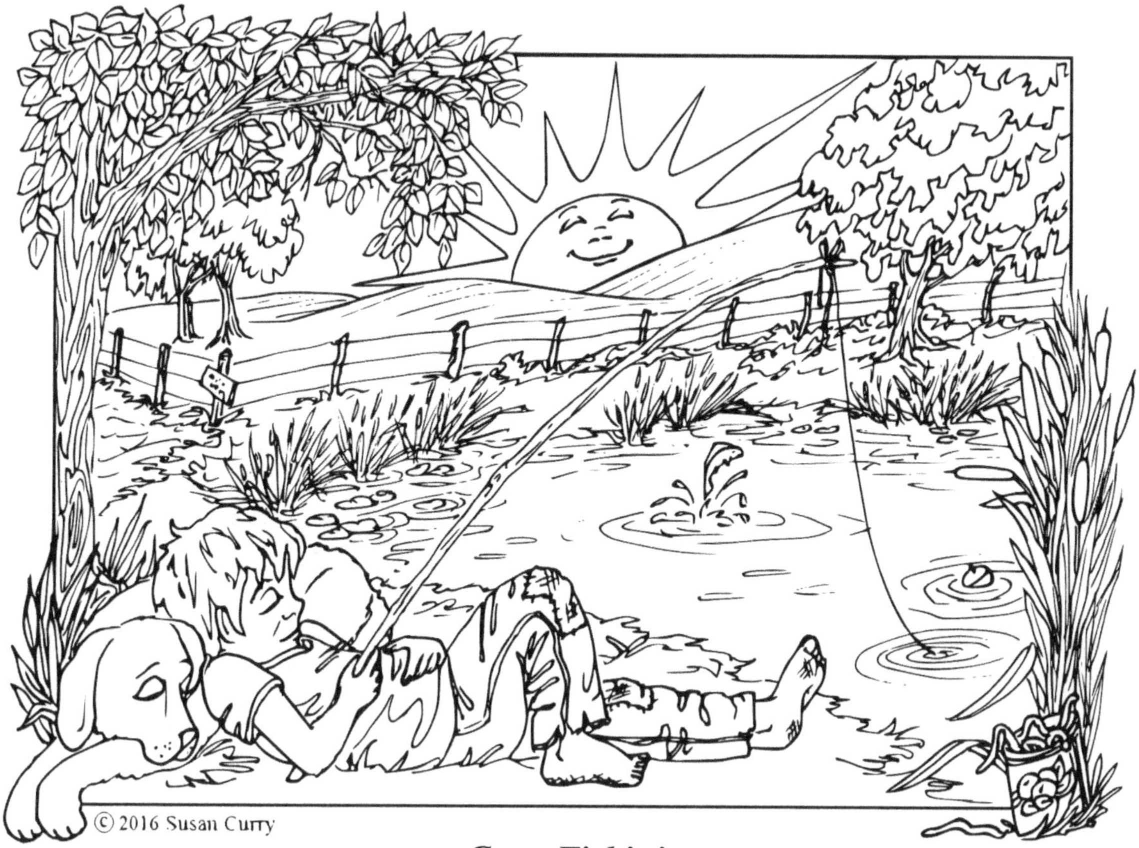

Gone Fishin'

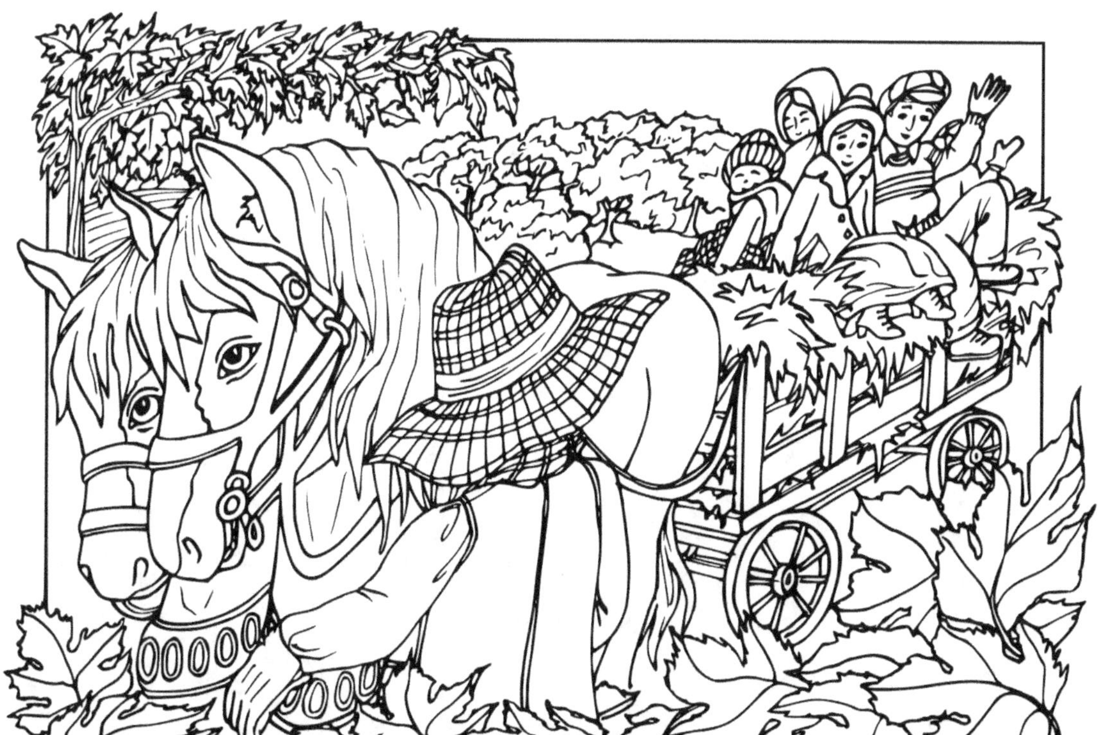

© 2016 Susan Curry

The Hay Ride

© 2016 Susan Curry

*"And the angel said unto them, Fear not: for, behold,
I bring you good tidings of great joy.."*

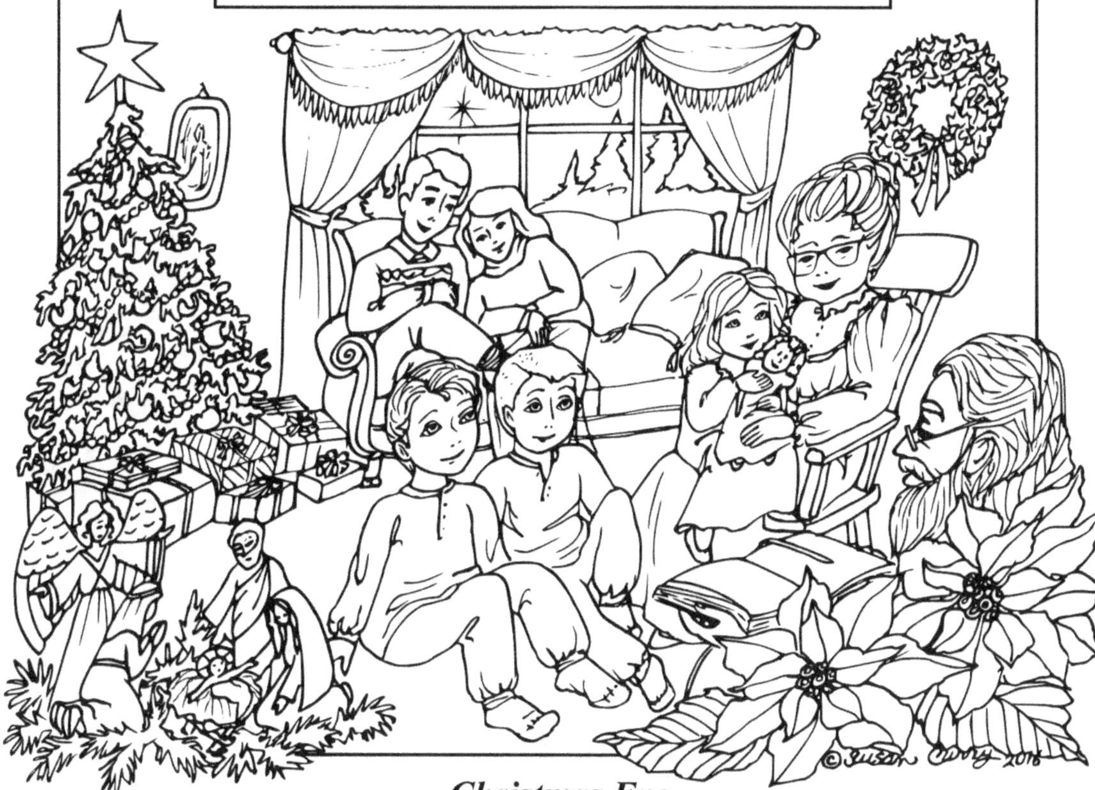

Christmas Eve

God bless the farmers who feed our world.

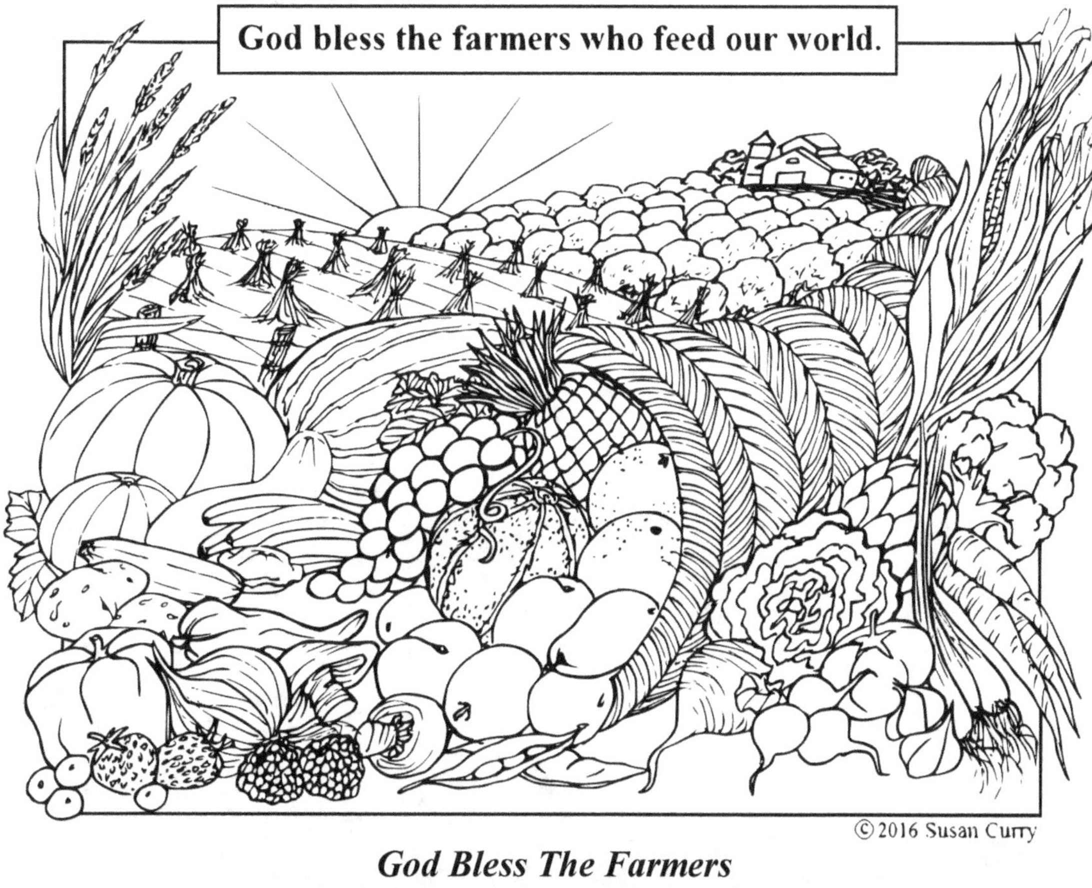

© 2016 Susan Curry

God Bless The Farmers

Living On Memory Lane - The Story Of The Drawings

Nana Sign In Page –

Nana is one of the people that are a part of this book and 'this story'. She is a little bit of my Australia grandmother, who we called 'Nana'…a bit of my own mother…and even a little of me.

The love of her life and mine is 'Papa'. Papa is the spitting image of my hubbie Ed. He is the bearded, old man in several of my drawings. Ed is lovely known as Papa to all of his kids, grandkids and me. Ed grew up on an 'old fashioned' dairy farm in the Central Valley of California and knows what it is like to live that kind of life. He had to get up in the middle of the night to help milk the cows, before heading to school.

The Scarecrow -

This picture was the first truly detailed drawing that I had created in years. I drew it, before I even knew that I was starting a coloring book. I received so many positive comments from my online friends about this picture. They encouraged and inspired me to begin drawing again...with a purpose.

This happy fellow is permanently employed on 'pest control' on a local farm. His 'sunny companion' makes sure that the corn crop is doing well.

The flower in the lower corner is a Brown Eyed Susan. My grandmother said that these bright yellow flowers were named for me, but I think that she just wanted me to like them as much as she did.

The Outhouse –

If you have never had to take a path from the house to that strange, little shed 'out back', then you have missed a real adventure. The outhouse was the original, enclosed toilet. My mom's name for the outhouse was 'dunny'. I don't know, if that was just an Aussie thing; but she often talked about her home in Australia and their dunny in the back yard.

Inside one of these little buildings, you found a wooden bench with one hole or two awaiting visitors in need. The smell was breathtaking and often drew everything from flies and spiders to other wild critters. In my drawing, I made sure that it was a time of year, when the flowers helped to perfume the air and add some color to drab, little building at the end of the pathway lined with stones.

The Attic -

Maybe I was just a weird kid, but I always loved going up into the attic of our home. I talked my parents into letting me 'spending the night' on the small area of wooden floor between the rafters.

Attics hold great memories. An old trunk can hold more treasure than a pirate's chest. I still remember the day that I opened the big trunk in our attic and found my Mom's wedding veil, old curling irons, a pair of beautiful opera glasses and lace gloves that didn't cover the fingers. Of course, there were photographs of the family going back many years...and so much, much more.

This drawing of Papa and Nana's attic hold many items which represent memories for me. The old stand up dress form, the doll house, the old chest, the lamps and train set were all part of our attic in my childhood home. Certainly, anyone with an attic has boxes, books and tangled Christmas tree lights tucked up under the rafters.

This attic also contains a precious, china head doll from the 1990's. That is a memory of a doll that was offered to me by a very sweet old lady, named Aunt Susie. It had been her doll, when she was growing up on a farm in South Dakota in the early 1900's. I declined to take that doll from Aunt Susie, because I knew that it held memories from her childhood. Sad to say, it ended up in a church rummage sale and sold for only one dollar. That broke my heart, because I would have treasured that doll, if only for the memory of its special owner.

Nana's Flower Garden -

Nana has some visitors to her flower garden today. The wild birds know that she is their friend.

Wild birds have always been very friendly with me. I have had wild birds actually land on me and follow me into my home. When I lived in Chula Vista, visitors to my rose nursery were shocked to see a Mexican blue jay land next to me and try to talk to me. That was Napolean ... my beautiful, feathered friend ... along with the hummingbirds, black birds, sparrows and doves.

The Peach Harvest -

I live in the Central Valley of California, surrounded by fields of corn, cotton and grapevines; but the orchards with their fruit and nut bearing trees produce equally important agricultural crops, including delicious peaches. This sweet, juicy fruit is a great for baking, canning and eating right off the tree. In my drawing, I made sure to include some favorite 'uses' for this popular fruit...including one big slice of peach pie.

Warning: This picture may give you a craving for peach pie, peach ice cream or some other peachy dessert. My hubbie's favorite is peach cobbler.

The Prize Winning Pig -

This drawing brings back a sweet memory of my son Brian. When he was about 7 years old, we took a trip to South Dakota and spent a week with Aunt Susie on her farm. Susie raised chickens, sheep and pigs. Brian loved every minute of the trip and became friends with the old farmhand named Frank.

On the day we were getting ready to head back to California, I was surprised at how quickly Brian got into our car. Then, I got in front seat and heard a strange sound...a little squeak...or should I say squeal coming from the back seat. I turned and looked at Brian. Guilt was all over his face.

Caught red handed, Brian blurted out, "Frank said that I could keep him."

Then, he opened his jacket and revealed a piglet...about 3 pounds of squealing pork on his lap. There was no way that we could keep that animal. This wasn't some pygmy, potbellied pig. This critter would all too quickly grow into an enormous, farm size hog. Aunt Susie and I both gave Frank a dirty look, as he took the piglet away from my teary eyed, little boy.

I later got Brian a guinea pig...something more realistic for a small boy in the suburbs of Southern California. That is as close as I want to come to having a pig in my house.

The Farmhouse -

During a road trip with my hubbie, I got my inspiration for Papa and Nana's house. There it was...a cute, little home that had obviously been part of a farm for many years. I liked the size of it, the single dormer in the roof...but what was that tall structure at the back. I knew that it wasn't a silo. Time to consult was my 'farm expert' and hubbie Ed.

Ed gave me the name for the strange building at the back of the small farmhouse. "That the pump house." I learned a lot about pump houses on the long ride down an old road with my hubbie. Ed explained the pump house was 'the shelter' for the huge, water tank that was located at the top of the building. Elevation of the tank was necessary to provided water pressure through gravity to the house; and the lower level of the pump house was a great, cold storage area for fruit, vegetables or even smoked meat. The other alternative use for the lower level was to make it into a tool shed.

In this drawing, Nana has gone to the porch to welcome company...maybe the grandkids. The farm dog is running to meet the visitors at the front gate.

The Barn -

On a back road near our home, I saw the remains of the old barn; and it spoke to me. I knew that the barn on Memory Lane would have to be the same style as the old, abandoned one...not some huge, red barn with 6 angles to the roof. No. I wanted a simple barn like the kind we see around our valley. That would be perfect for Papa's farm.

As for a farm truck, I just remembered Ed's most important rule for a vehicle..."It has got to have character." What is character? That's simple. If the truck is old, dirty inside and out, dented, scratched up and rusty...it has 'character'. Ed prides himself on giving character to his vehicles. From the first month that we were married, Ed has been putting 'character' into our vehicles. (Groan)

I never tried to draw a truck or any other vehicle, until I started these pictures for this coloring book. I surprised myself; and even my Ed was very impressed, as he explained that Chevy stopped making split windshields in 1950. How do men remember such trivial things about car and trucks, but they can't retain far more important things?

Laundry Day -

Nana is the mother hanging clothes out on the 'line' to dry. One of her babies (probably my Mom) is sitting on her blanket nearby, playing with clothespins. Someone drew faces on the clothespins to make them look like little people; and now, they are a perfect toy for this baby to enjoy.

Now days, we have washing machines and dryers that make laundry relatively a simple task. I am old enough to remember, when laundry involved many hours of hard work, especially if there were babies in the family. I even had the 'pleasure' of using a wringer washing machine for a while, back in the 1960's. It was a dangerous machine to use, as the wet pieces of wash had to be fed through rollers which would squeeze out the excess water. Fingers which happened to get too close to the rollers would be 'injured' and require mending. Buttons which were not carefully folded inside the wet shirt would be instantly popped off the shirt, which would also require mending later.

Hanging clothes on the clothesline was back breaking work, and it was only part of the laundry process. Laundry day started at the sink, scrubbing some stain out of clothes, before you put them into the latest appliance...the wringer washing machine. The tub held the warm soapy water and (like modern washing machines) churned the clothing for a while, until you turned off the tub and activated the wringer apparatus on top of the noisy appliance.

Listening To The Radio -

There was no television or the computers of any kind, back in the early 1900's. The phonograph had found its place in many homes; but the real change in family life occurred, when radio became affordable for the average homeowner. At that moment, the outside world became a living part of our homes.

In this drawing, Papa and Nana are doing more than just read the newspaper and knitting. They are listening to that beautiful, new radio, while a kitten playfully unravels Nana's yarn across the living room floor.

The research for this drawing was fun and led me do a small modification to a 'Tiffany style' lamp. By the way, I am a fan of Tiffany lamps; and I have Tiffany 'style' lamps in my dining room and bedroom.

I let my hubbie Ed help me choose which radio to use in my drawing, as he told me about the old radio (like the one in this picture) that his Papa kept in barn on the dairy farm where they lived. Ed told me that his dad couldn't afford a newspaper subscription, but he liked to listen to the news on the radio, while he milked the cows. We have a replica of this style radio which Ed loves to use.

The General Store -

In the summer of 1957, I got to spend a couple of months with a girlfriend and her family at their vacation home in the mountains of California...in one of the smallest towns that I have ever seen. It was called Sierra City. It had been an old Pony Express stop and then a Wells Fargo stop along the way to San Francisco.

It was in Sierra City that I saw my first, real general store. The very old and very small building held the only store in town. In fact...it seemed to be the only business in Sierra City. It was also the gas station, post office and main gathering place for the community. The owner/clerk was the town's mayor, postman and probably held 5 more titles.

Maybe a dozen families had homes in that remote town. Summer brought fishermen who would come up to try their luck in the beautiful streams nearby. Some scout groups came up to camp among the trees, but that was it.

There were no televisions and the radio was a few country stations, at a time when rock and roll was my thing. So, visiting the general store was an almost daily event for the townsfolk, including the visiting teenager from Southern California. That's where you went for everything from sodas and candy to the news of the world and the best gossip on the mountain.

Sweet Adeline -

How many of you are familiar with the classic, barber shop quartet song from the 1920's entitled 'Sweet Adeline'? As I created this drawing, I found myself singing the words to that sweet, old song…

"Sweet Adeline (sung as Ad-Ooo-liine)…my Adeline. At night, dear heart…for you I pine. In all my dreams, your fair face beams. You're the flower of my heart…Sweet Adeline."

This drawing was inspired by a recent trip to a barber shop with my hubbie Ed who bears a strong resemblance to the bearded gentleman in the barber's chair. The scene is obvious. Papa has joined in the harmonizing with 3 barbers and a pack dogs outside the shop. In my mind, they are singing (or howling) at the top of their lungs to that old song 'Sweet Adeline'.

By the way, my hubbie Ed cannot (as the old expression goes) 'carry a tune in a bucket'. He is the only person I know that was asked to NOT SING in church, by a pastor who insisted, "Everyone sing...except Ed." Ed's concept of singing is more akin to the howling of a hound dog; and when he can't remember the words to a song, he makes up his own words...often inappropriate to the occasion. :)

The Party Dress -

As I sketched this picture, a story developed. First, there was the young shopper, trying on a new dress. Then, I added her mother who would be paying for the purchase...if the dress was appropriate for her teenager who is growing into a woman 'a bit too soon'...in Mom's opinion.

The window shopper is a more modern woman, who is showing interest in that new style suit in the window. Maybe she will be able to afford it in a month or two, if she really 'watches her pennies'. It costs almost a week's salary.

The last character in this vignette is the older sales lady, who is probably also the owner and seamstress in the very small but popular, ladies shop. This was the drawing in which I created the character who would become Nana in the rest of my story, because she reminded me of my Nana who did so much sewing in her lifetime.

The unique piece of jewelry in the display case that looks like a magnifying glass is called a lonquette. It really is a magnifying glass...a gorgeous one on a long chain. Proper ladies in the past would wear a lonquette as jewelry; but it was also an important visual aid, when glasses were considered very unattractive on a woman's face.

I own a beautifully, bejeweled lonquette and love to wear it, when I get all dressed up for a special occasion.

The Barn Dance

A barn dance was a social event for most country towns back in the old days. A local farmer and his neighbors would work together to tidy up the barn, string up some lights and call on the services of the best fiddler and square dance caller in the county.

The young ladies of the community would put on their brightest dresses and petticoats, in the hope of making a good impression and catching the attention of one of the young men. Married folks already had their dance partners for the night.

Even the youngest kids could come along to watch the grownups doosy doo around the floor of the barn to some good, foot stomping music.

The Covered Bridge -

There are many covered bridges in the United States, especially in areas that receive snow in the winter. They are beautiful reminders of our historic past.

I saw my first covered bridge, when I visited the famous Gettysburg National Park, the site of one of the largest battles during the Civil War. I was stuck by the beauty of the large structure spanning a slow moving stream. At the time, I didn't realize that it was Sachs Covered Bridge, one of America's most well-known, haunted places.

In this picture, a farmer is taking a load of hay by wagon...somewhere...maybe to share with a neighbor. You can almost hear the clip clop of the horse's hooves as he trots across the wooden flooring of the bridge. The water below the covered bridge makes a wonderful sound, as it cascades over the boulders and drops into a large pool, before moving onward.

The time is early summer, and daisies are abundantly blooming along the river that passes slowly through the valley. Butterflies and lady bugs are almost as numerous as flowers that cover the grassy slopes of the river.

The Wedding Day -

The little bride is Cecelia Newton Panton who has just married Charles Panton. The year is 1920. Cecelia would become the mother of 5 children, 'Nana' to a couple of dozen grandchildren. I am the eldest of all those grandkids. Most of Nana and Charlie Panton's grandchildren are now grandparents themselves. All total...Charlie and Cecelia's family has grown to more than 100, as their great-great grandchildren are now becoming parents themselves. We are spread out across Australia and America; but we all can trace our roots back to that wedding day.

Call it artistic license; but in this drawing, I brought my Australian grandparents to Memory Lane, which in mind is somewhere in the Central Valley of California. In truth, my grandparents were married in Kalgoorlie, West Australia and never lived in America...though they visited their war bride daughters and their families in the States on several occasions.

Each of their visits to their America gave me the opportunity to learn more about my family history. During Nana's last visit in 1974, she shared with me the stories of her courtship and marriage to my grandfather, her life as young mother in the bush country of West Australia, and even giving birth in their 'bush country home' with the assistance of a midwife (called 'a sister', though they were not of any religious order).

Warm Cookies -

What person doesn't have a wonderful memory of warm cookies? That incredible aroma coming from the kitchen was impossible to ignore.

My boys loved my warm sugar cookies. They would be 'sneaking them' off of the counter, before they had time to cool down. My recipe was one that I got from my first cookbook, Betty Crockers Cookbook for Children. How easy can you get? I had to quadruple the recipe every time I made them or have no cookies left by the next day.

In this picture, Nana has a couple of grandkids over to the farm to help with her baking today. Little Sister is helping mix the cookie dough...and lick the spoon. Little Brother is in charge of cookie testing. Nana's hubbie and the love of her life (Papa) is making sure to 'kiss the cook', as he grabs a warm cookie.

Note: The tall cupboard at the back of the kitchen is called a 'Hoosier cabinet'. This tall piece of kitchen furniture had a flour bin built into the upper cabinet with a hand cranked sifter at the bottom. Nana only has to place her bowl on the counter below the bin and turn the crank to get flour ready for her baking.

The Hoosier usually held baking tools, spices and more. It was a must have for any lady who liked to bake...back in the day.

The Sewing Basket -

This hand drawn picture takes me back to my youth, when every young lady was expected to know how to sew, knit, crochet, embroider and even darn socks. That usually meant that she owned one of these beautiful baskets to hold her smaller supplies, like spools of threads, buttons and her darning egg.

The darning egg is the wooden ball on a handle. A sock needing repair was slipped over the egg; then, it could be mended with yarn. Most folks don't know how to do that anymore. They just say 'Darn!' and buy new socks. (chuckling to self)

I hope that this drawing will allow your imagination to run wild with colors of yarn, thread and all those familiar items. There are so many good memories in this picture.

The Quilting Bee -

Now, doesn't this look like fun?

In this drawing, several generations of family members and friends have joined together in a 'Quilting Bee'. The ladies took up positions around the large wooden frame that held the fabric stretched out across 2 long rollers which took up the slack, as the members of the quilting bee added stitches around the individual pieces of fabric. This was a long, slow possession...even with a talented group of ladies sewing for many hours. The end result was a beautiful 'work of art' made of many colored pieces of fabric.

A quilt like this would be given to a special friend or member of the family and be handed down from one generation to the next for many, many years. Sometimes, it might even carry the history of the family or people who made it.

The best part of the quilting bee was the fellowship and stories shared around the quilt. It was also a time to teach the younger members of a family the 'secrets' to make a good quilt. Youngsters were encouraged to try and make the tiny stitches for a quilt that might even go on their bed or be handed down to them in the future...along with the memories of the people who hands created this precious keepsake. Quilts are beautiful works of art, and you might even see them displayed on a wall rather than a bed. Museums and collectors prize these treasures from the past and their detailed artistry.

The Vintage Bathroom -

As a youngster, I spent one day each week with my paternal grandmother who lived in a small, very old house that still had the original, claw-foot bathtub. I looked forward to taking bubble baths in that 'huge tub'. I could barely see over the rim, when I was sitting neck deep in warm water and bubbles. Soaking in one of those old time bathtubs leaves pleasant memories that last a lifetime.

I am also familiar with those toilets with the elevated water tank and a pull chain flush. Aunt Susie had one in her basement on a farm in South Dakota; but it was only used in winter, when the path to the outhouse was deep in snow. I couldn't resist pulling the chain, when I was down in the basement...even though it was summertime.

I actually owned a crystal powder bowl and perfume atomizer like the ones in the foreground of this picture. There is something about 'fluffing on powder with a powder puff' or 'squeezing the bulb of the atomizer' to apply perfume that is different and seems more elegant than using modern powder and spray on perfume. These items invite you to 'step back in time'.

Gone Fishin' -

Fishing is still a favorite way for so many folks to relax and escape from work, responsibilities and stress of modern life. A fishing pole, your best friend and a can of worms was all you needed, back in the good 'ole days. You knew the spot 'where they were biting'...in the pond at the end of the dirt road.

This youngster couldn't be happier, as he and his dog take a nap on this beautiful day. In the shade of a tree with his line in the murky water of the pond, catching fish was the plan; but it wasn't required to have a good time. You could always tell some 'fish story' about 'the one that got away', when you got home.

The Hay Ride -

The driver of the hay wagon takes a moment to check on his team, before he takes a load of hay and some happy passengers on a ride through the country side on a chilly, Autumn day...or evening, depending on how you see it.

I began this drawing with those 2 horses. That felt so strange to me, because "I don't draw horses."...or do I? After a lot of research on hay rides, I made a couple of 'start up sketches', but I kept trying to put the emphasis on the hay wagon and hide the horses.

It wasn't, until I saw one photo of the most beautiful team of horses that I found my inspiration. I could finally 'put the horses before the cart'...or wagon in this case.

Christmas Eve -

I spent my first Christmas after marrying Ed with his family. It was while I was with those remarkable people that I witnessed the most wonderful, family tradition and really discovered Christmas.

After sharing in the huge, holiday feast, everyone (and I mean old and young) gathered in the living room. As if on cue, the room became quiet and the oldest member of the family (Papa Curry...Ed's dad who was 87 at the time) picked up his Bible; and he began to read the story of the birth of Jesus.

Truthfully, it was a surprise to me that 'people actually did this...at Christmas time'. I was raised with the 'happy holidays' version of Christmas. We always had a tree, lots of presents and holiday treats of course. I grew up with tales of Santa Claus and hung up my stocking every year. We didn't talk about Jesus, though I knew all the Christmas carols. I even knew the story of Jesus...well...sort of; but this was something quite different for me.

The spirit in that room on Christmas Eve with Ed's family, the attentiveness of every person to the words being spoken, the sense of wonder at the story that they all knew so well was inspiring and wondrous to me. That year...that moment...was my 'first real Christmas'.

God Bless The Farmers -

Where I live now in the Central Valley of California is farm land. Wherever I travel in this area, I see vineyards, orchards and fields. We are one of the largest farming areas in America...for sure in California.

I am well aware that our farmers are struggling right now with problems from drought to the decreasing prices for their crops. They are in trouble, and their fertile land is quickly being sold off to make room for more tract homes and shopping centers. We are losing 'a way of life' as fewer young people are getting the training and knowledge to 'take up the plow' and the burden of growing the crops that our nation and the world required.

This drawing salutes those great people who grow the food that we need each day to survive.

BONUS PAGE

A Preview of my next book, entitled 'The Adventures of Little Sister'.

Dressing Up -

This drawing of 'Little Sister' reminds me of my younger sister Debbie in so many ways. She loved to dress up and play with Mom's jewelry. She was always the 'girlie girl' in our family. Not surprising, my now grown up, kid sister still loves and collects dolls. Deb also repairs vintage purses, like the one in this drawing. She can repair the finest details in those delicate, beaded bags and give them new life.

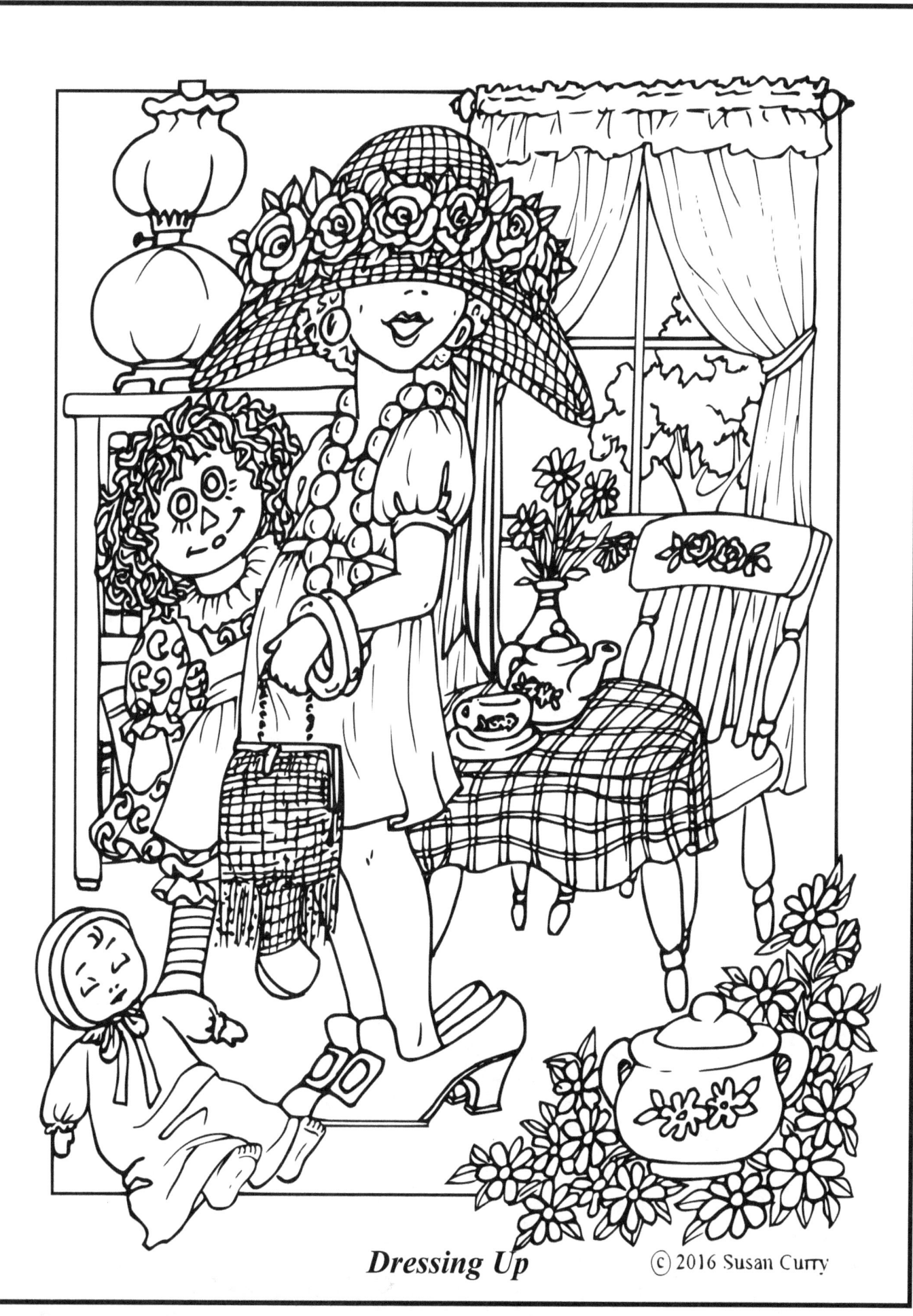

Dressing Up   © 2016 Susan Curry